My Grandmother's House

By Kathy Lacey Sellers

This is a work of fiction based on true events in History. Any resemblance to anyone alive or dead is purely coincidental.

All rights reserved. Published by Sleepytown Press.

Sleepytown Press and its associated logos are trademarks of Sleepytown Press.

No part of this publication may be reproduced or used in any form without the prior written permission of the author and publisher.

© 2017 by Kathy Lacey Sellers

ISBN: 978-1-937260-29-3

Cover by Dale Price

Sleepytown Press

www.sleepytownpress.com

Dedication

I write because I cannot sing

Dedicated to My Darling, Richard; you are my inspiration and my encouragement.

Special thanks to Lori, Dee Dee, and my sister, Nonnie; I could not do what I do without your help.

Deuteronomy 29:29
The secret things belong unto the LORD our God: but those things, which are revealed, belong unto us and to our children forever, that we may do all the words of the law.

Proverbs 10: 11-12
The mouth of a righteous man is a well of life but violence covereth the mouth of the wicked.
Hatred stirreth up strife, but love covereth all sins.

1 John 2:16
For all that is in the world, the lust of the flesh, the lust of the eyes, and the pride of life, is not from the Father, but is from the world.

Chapter 1

Her mother pulled the car off the highway, opened the door and told Katherine to slide across the seat. She helped her daughter out and then led the way through the tall weeds and across the damp, marsh-like clump of land that served as a barricade to all except the truly determined visitor. The young girl held tightly to her mother's hand and dutifully followed her to a group of clustered tree limbs, offering a cool, refreshing shade from the early summer sun. The canopy filtered out most of the light and darkened the path, which made it necessary for them to wait momentarily so their eyes could adjust. Once their pupils dilated, they could see the old dirt pathway that had been the original road to her grandmother's house. Many years of neglect, due to the new paved highway, had caused the road to dwindle down to nothing more than a trail full of ruts and patches of grass and weeds.

Encouraged by her mother's gentle voice, assuring her that the shortcut was much quicker, Katherine released her grip and continued the journey until they stopped halfway up the hill to catch their breath. Her mother took her white lace handkerchief out from her small handbag and blotted her forehead and then fanned her face.

It was very unusual to see Elizabeth Anne Langford perspire. She was a true Southern lady who took much pride in her appearance. Her dark shoulder-length hair was pulled back into a ponytail with a ribbon that matched her pale blue dress. Her choice of pocketbook and shoes complimented her outfit and her tanned, smooth skin made her an object of much admiration and envy. Katherine's father often referred to his wife as, "A vision of beauty."

Although many people agreed with his assessment, her seemingly effortless beauty did not happen without enhancement from her endless collection of paints, creams and lotions, nor did it happen instantly. From start to finish, her beauty routine could take up to an hour or longer. Katherine was fascinated by the process but not to the point of aspiring to become a duplicate of her mother when she grew up.

"I'm parched," Elizabeth Anne panted. "I bet your grandmother will have a large pitcher of ice water waiting for us." She moistened her lips and motioned for her daughter to follow her.

"I hope so," Katherine answered. The thought of a refreshing glass of ice water made her push forward. She could feel the muscles in her legs tighten as they pulled her up the steep hill. She was anxious to reach her grandmother's house and was certainly not disappointed when she saw an old, black gentleman, wearing overalls and a straw hat, coming toward them with a bucket of water.

"Miss Beff Anne," he shouted. "I figured you and the little missy would be getting here bout now." He held up the dipper and said, "I also figured y'all would be thirsty, too."

"God bless you, Mr. Dodie," Katherine's mother shouted back. She picked up her pace and so did Katherine.

The water bucket was like a magnet, drawing her poor, tired feet toward it, forcing them to go faster. She looked down and discovered, to her horror, that dust had covered her brand new, Yancey Department Store, dress shoes. Her heart fluttered, almost causing panic until she noticed her mother's shoes were covered with dust as well. That revelation gave her a sense of confidence. Surely she wouldn't receive a scolding for being untidy once her mother discovered they both shared the same affliction; unsightly dust covered shoes.

Katherine waited until after her mother had wet her handkerchief and dabbed the back of her neck, then she reached for the dipper and took a big drink. She swished the water around in her mouth, leaned her head backward and allowed the cool wetness to trickle down her throat. "Ahh," she sighed and then handed the dipper to her mother.

"Dat there is fresh from the well. Should be good and cold," the old gentleman said, with a wide grin.

"Oh, Mr. Dodie, you're an angel…an angel straight from heaven." Elizabeth Anne spoke between sips. "I dare say I was about to faint." She waved her handkerchief and heaved a sigh of relief. "Do you mind if we rest a moment before tackling the rest of the hill?"

"Not at all, Miss Beff Anne, not at all." He set the bucket down. "It will give us a chance to catch up."

Katherine listened as Mr. Dodie and her mother laughed and carried on about things that had happened when she was a child. He teased her about being skinny-legged and freckled-faced and she teased him about the time the hog got loose and rooted up the turnip patch.

Katherine found their conversation entertaining and informative. She discovered things about her mother that she had not known before, things that made her less perfect, but more endearing. Katherine loved and admired her mother, but she was a little intimidated by her, wondering if she could ever measure up. This intimate insight into her mother's past relieved some of her dread. It was good to hear her mother laugh. She truly seemed to be enjoying herself, even after the rest period ended and as they labored their way to their final destination.

Katherine Hobbs Carter stood on her front porch, fumbled with her apron a few seconds before abandoning the idea of removing it, and then she swiftly walked down the steps and across the wide, neatly groomed yard toward her daughter and granddaughter. "Elizabeth Anne," she shouted, with her arms stretched wide.

The loud announcement of their arrival disturbed the chickens in the chicken coop and caused them to cackle and flap their wings so loudly it woke up the sleeping hound dog under the porch steps. He crawled out, shook himself off, focused his attention on the strangers and then started growling and snarling at them.

Katherine and her mother were frightened. They stood still.

"Here!" Mr. Dodie shouted. "Hush up, Jake. Dees folks ain't gonna hurt nothing. You hush up!"

The dog immediately stopped his daunting display of terror and wagged his tail, setting Elizabeth Anne's mind at ease. She ran toward her mother, threw her arms around her and started laughing and crying at the same time. It took several minutes for Katherine's grandmother to notice her. She waved her over.

"And this is my sweet granddaughter, I bet you don't even remember me," she said, bending down and gently pushing back the hair that had worked out from her braids. "You were two years old the last time I saw you."

Katherine smiled and straightened her shoulders. She was amazed that this lovely lady was her grandmother. She wasn't anything like the image she had envisioned; no gray hair tightly weaved into a bun or crow's feet clustered around her eyes. Her skin was wrinkle free and youthful, she could have easily been mistaken for someone half her age.

"My goodness." Her grandmother's voice wavered. "You're the spitting image of your mother when she was your age."

"Dats zackly what I thought, too," Mr. Dodie chimed in. "She's purdie as a picture. The little missy looks just like her mama."

"My name is Katherine, just like yours." Katherine looked at her grandmother. "I was named after you."

"Yes, indeed you were and I'm very proud of that fact." Her grandmother's eyes glistened with tears. "I am very proud and honored," she said. "Proud to have you as my granddaughter and honored if you would call me, Grandmother Kate." She stood up. "What would you like me to call you? Should I call you Katherine or maybe Katie?"

"Katherine is fine." She paused, lowering her head. "My parents insist that I be called Katherine, but…I like what Mr. Dodie calls me." She looked at her mother with anxious eyes. "Please, may I be called Little Missy?"

Her mother hesitated. "Katherine, I don't…"

"Please, Mother, please." Katherine interrupted. "Mr. Dodie calls you Beff Anne. Please let me be called Little Missy."

"All southern belles need a pet name," Grandmother Kate said hastily. "Your father called you Sweet Pea, remember? And Dodie and Odessa…"

Katherine's mother raised her hands, halting the protest. "Okay, I suppose Little Missy will be acceptable for a term of endearment but it is not to replace your official name." She looked at her daughter sternly. "You understand?"

"Yes, ma'am." Katherine reached for her grandmother's hand and walked with her toward the old faded antebellum.

Many years of the hot Alabama sun had robbed the house of its bright white color and had replaced it with a weathered-worn dull shade of gray. The home was well maintained, standing stately and proud in spite of its age. Two huge magnolia trees stood on either side of the front steps and there were four rocking chairs on the wraparound porch. A straight back chair, a table and a potted fern set next to the front door.

"Lets go to the kitchen and check on dinner," Grandmother Kate said, leading the way inside, through the foyer and down the hall. The smell of fried chicken and apple pie overpowered Katherine and made her stomach growl out loud. She followed behind the adults until she got to the parlor and then something caught her eye. Hanging over the fireplace mantel was a large calendar with a picture of a beautiful yellow cat, a basket of pink, purple, and blue flowers, big letters that spelled out M-A-Y and the numbers 1-9-5-4 in big bold print. Katherine admired the calendar even though she knew her mother would never allow anything that simple to hang in her elegant home. It was far too common to be displayed on the Langford walls but Katherine found it to be appealing and reminiscent of a nursery rhyme she had read years ago when she was first learning to read.

At five years old she had been able to read, write, and recite the alphabet from A to Z, and count all the way up to one hundred. Her learning process had begun at an early age when her parents enrolled her into a private enrichment program and had continued after her family moved and she had been accepted into Stockton Academy, the best private elementary school in Atlanta, Georgia. Katherine was proud of her academic achievements, but she was not boastful. Her parents and teachers had instilled in her that pride could be a good attribute, prompting her to always put forth her best efforts, but they also cautioned her that pride could become destructive and all consuming. She was mindful not to brag or put on airs.

Next to the cat calendar was a tall black clock that ticked very loudly, a large box of matches, and a bud vase with roses etched into the glass. Across from the fireplace were a couch and two chairs with crocheted doilies spread across the arms, and behind the parlor door was a lamp table, stacked high with books, one of which was an old leather-bound Bible. Hanging directly on the wall above the Bible was a picture of Jesus standing outside a house. He appeared to be knocking on the door and He had a sad, somber expression on His face.

"So here you are," Grandmother Kate said, poking her head inside the room. "I wondered where you disappeared to."

"I was just looking," Katherine stammered. "I didn't touch anything, I promise."

"Well, it would be okay if you did," her grandmother said. "There is nothing untouchable here." She pulled her granddaughter close. "This house is full of love. Everything in it has either been given to me by a loved one or is here because it reminds me of something or someone I love." She pointed toward the old clock. "That was a Christmas present from your Grandfather Carter. He ordered it from a catalog and had it shipped all the way from Germany and that lamp table was my mother's and so was that Bible."

"What about that cat calendar?" Katherine asked. "Who gave you that?"

"Nobody; I bought it for myself because I love cats."

"You do?" she asked. "I love cats too…but Mother won't let me have one because they shed."

"Your mother had a cat when she was little." Grandmother Kate looked sideways at her granddaughter and smiled. "She called it Tom until it surprised us one day and gave birth to four black and white kittens; after that, she changed its name to Duchess."

"Duchess," Katherine replied. "That's funny."

"Indeed it is." Grandmother Kate nodded. "And you know what else is funny?" she asked.

Katherine shook her head.

"You and me in here rather than in the kitchen eating fried chicken, homemade biscuits and apple pie." She walked toward the door and asked, "Are you hungry?"

"Yes ma'am," Katherine said politely and followed her down the hall.

Chapter 2

The hallway was full of family portraits. Several of them were old and faded and of people Katherine had no idea who they were. There was one of her grandmother, and her mother when she was little, standing in front of the Hollinsville Train Station. Her grandmother's hair was piled high on top of her head, she wore a cream colored dress and a hat with feathers sticking up on the side. Her mother was holding a rag doll in one hand and a tiny pocketbook in the other. They were either going somewhere or coming back from somewhere because there were three suitcases setting beside them. Katherine was curious about the picture but not enough to stop and ask.

When they finally made their way to the kitchen, which was at the very back of the house, her mother looked up and inquired, "Did you get lost?"

"No, just distracted," Katherine answered. Her intention was to explain her distraction by mentioning the parlor and the cat calendar, but her mother handed her some plates and some silverware.

"Be a dear and set the table," she said, pointing to the small round table on the back screened-in porch. "It's so hot, we'll eat out there," she told her daughter and then she called out, " Miss Odessa, where are the glasses?"

"Who's Miss Odessa?" Katherine asked.

"Dat would be me, child." A very large black woman came out from the butler's pantry carrying a huge bowl of mashed potatoes. "I be Dodie's wife and I also be the cook," she said, stopping long enough to give Katherine a good looking over. "Ah, ain't you a purdie thang?" She smiled a big, wide smile that revealed plump cheeks, deep dimples and straight, pearly white teeth. She clutched her chest and whispered. "You look jest like your mama when she was a girl." She swapped glances from daughter to mother. "I swear, Miss Beff

Anne, it's like stepping back in time."

"Don't you get nostalgic on me, Miss Odessa." Katherine's mother beamed with pride. "It's been a long time since I was twelve."

"It seems like yesterdee." She shook her head and breathed deeply, "It's hard to imagine, but it's true, you're all growed up with a young'un of your own." Miss Odessa waved her hand in front of her face. "You're making me old, Miss Beff Anne, and forgetful. I can't even remember what I came in here for."

"Glasses." Katherine spoke up. "Mother asked you about the glasses."

"Oh, dat's right." Miss Odessa opened the cabinet door and pointed to the large glasses with tulips painted on them. "Use dees, Miss Beff Anne," she said. "Dey be big enough so we won't be having to refill dem every few minutes."

Katherine tagged along behind Miss Odessa and set the plain white dishes on the gray vinyl tablecloth that had cattails and dragonflies on it. Miss Odessa placed the mashed potatoes between the bowls of black-eyed peas and fried okra. Katherine's mother brought the glasses and the pitcher of sweet tea and her grandmother followed with the napkins and serving spoons.

Mr. Dodie came in from the garden, opened the screen door and held up two red-ripe tomatoes. "I'll have dees washed and sliced afore y'all finish setting the table," he said.

"Den you best be hurrying up," Miss Odessa told him, placing the spoons and forks next to the plates. "I've been cooking all morning and I'm hungrier than a she bear coming out of hibernation."

"Me too," Katherine stated, giving no thought to the fact that she had no idea how hungry that was.

Her grandmother laughed and pointed to the chair on the backside of the table. She quickly sat down and patiently waited until everybody was seated and the blessing was said; then she took a heaping spoonful from every bowl as it was passed around.

She piled her plate with mashed potatoes and gravy, fried okra, corn cut off the cob, and black-eyed peas. She put a chicken leg and a biscuit on her napkin because there was no more room on her plate, but she didn't take a slice of tomato because she wasn't particularly fond of them and besides that, she knew she had to save room for dessert.

Because her mother was such a staunch believer in moderation, Katherine was afraid she might remind her about gluttony being a sin so she lowered her head and purposely avoided looking in her mother's direction, just in case she was to notice the over abundance of food she had placed on her plate.

Katherine realized she sinned enough without trying, she surely didn't want it pointed out that she was sinning on purpose so she quietly asked God to forgive her and reminded Him that it would be down right rude and insulting to Miss Odessa and her grandmother if she didn't heartily partake of the delicious food they had worked so hard to prepare.

As soon as she finished her conversation with the good Lord, she quickly glanced at her mother, to make sure she wasn't giving her one of her disapproving stares, but she shouldn't have been concerned because her mother was busy explaining to Miss Odessa that she was watching her weight.

"Well, I can see every bone in your body, Miss Beff Anne." Miss Odessa raised her eyebrows. "If you watch your weight much more you're bound to dry up and blow away." She used the back of her spoon to form a hole in her mashed potatoes and then filled it with gravy. "You and the little missy need to put some meat on your bones," she said, placing the gravy bowl back on the table. She rolled her eyes toward her husband, smiled and said, "I don't worry too much bout my weight or watching my figure, I leave all dat up to Dodie."

Mr. Dodie laughed out loud, licked his fingers and then wiped the grease off his chin. "You look fine to me, Odessa, mighty fine," he said, reaching for another piece of fried chicken. "Any woman dat can cook like dis sho don't need no improvement."

"I'm glad you feel dat way," she replied. "Cause there's so much of me to watch, I wouldn't want to over burden you."

All the adults laughed, even Katherine's mother, so she figured it was safe for her to indulge and enjoy. And enjoy she did. By the time she got around to dessert she barely had any room left. She was trying to decide if she wanted to eat her pie or if she wanted to save it for later when a young, dark haired boy knocked on the screen door.

"Mrs. Carter, it's me," he called. "It's James Everett, can I come in?"

Grandmother Kate turned around and motioned for him to enter. "James Everett, come on in here and have some dinner with us," she said, making room for him at the table.

"Oh, no ma'am. I just come to let you know that me and Travis are here to deliver the lumber." He opened the door, looked at the table and then he hung his head and stared at the floor. "Travis sent me to ask you where you want us to unload the truck," he said shyly.

"That can wait, honey. Come, sit down and have something to eat," Grandmother Kate insisted. "We'll call your brother too."

He glanced up at the food and stared lustfully for a brief moment but then quickly looked away and shook his head. "No thank you. I ain't…we ain't hungry." He stepped inside but kept his hand on the door handle. "I don't mean to interrupt your meal," he said, looking at Mr. Dodie. "You want us to unload out back of the barn?" He lowered his head again and shifted his bare feet back and forth.

Katherine wondered where his shoes were, why he was walking around barefoot and why he didn't have a bandage on his big left toe. It appeared as if he had stumped it some time ago but hadn't taken the time to wipe off the blood; it had already started to dry and crust over. She reckoned the young boy's mother wasn't as nervous about germs as her mother was, because if that had been her toe, her mother would have had it washed, ointment on it and wrapped up like a mummy in a matter of a few seconds. And she would have given several lectures on blood poison, gangrene and the importance of good hygiene. Katherine didn't want to panic her mother or cause undue embarrassment to their visitor, so she decided not to mention his toe. She was relieved when Mr. Dodie pushed away from the table.

"Wrap the boys up some food, Odessa, dey can take it with dem." He winked at James Everett. "Come on and I'll show you where we gonna put the lumber," he said, picking up his straw hat.

The young boy looked up, smiled and scooted out the door and down the back steps. Katherine watched as he and Mr. Dodie walked to the side yard.

    Miss Odessa quickly wrapped up some chicken and biscuits. Grandmother Kate put two large slices of apple pie into a brown paper bag then she said, "I feel so sorry for Mary Ruth and her children. Wiley Holloway battled the evils of alcohol his entire life, but at least he did provide for his family. Now that he's dead, poor Mary Ruth has the burden of raising all six children by herself."

    Miss Odessa nodded in agreement. "I don't know what she'd do without Travis and Jo Nell. Dey done went out and got demselves a job so dey could help with the bills." She shook her head. "It's a shame what happened to Wiley."

    Katherine's curiosity got the better of her and before she could stop herself, she spit the words right out of her mouth, "What happen to Wiley? How did he die?"

    Her mother immediately shushed her. "You shouldn't ask such questions."

    "I'm sorry," she said, looking at her mother and then at her grandmother.

    "That's okay." Grandmother Kate patted her arm. "We shouldn't have been talking about other people's calamities anyway." She handed Katherine the bag. "Take this to James Everett."

    Katherine hurriedly took the paper sack and walked out the screened-in porch and down the steps. She could see Mr. Dodie and the boys unloading the lumber and stacking it under the overhang of the well house.

    "Hey, boy," she yelled.

    James Everett left the others and met her under the small oak tree next to the cellar door. She handed him the bag.

    "I ain't supposed to take no handouts." He pushed the bag away. "Travis says we have to make our own way."

    "This isn't a handout," Katherine stated. "It's a gift. My grandmother will be offended if you don't take it." She defiantly pushed the bag toward him. "Why are you acting this way? Don't you believe in people doing a good deed?"

    "Of course I do, but…"

    "But what?" Katherine interrupted. "A good deed needs to be

appreciated not prevented." She turned her head to the side and smiled. "I've heard my father say that a million times."

"Do you always repeat what your daddy says?" James Everett looked around to see if his brother was watching. "A good deed is only a good deed if there is a need." He stepped forward and whispered, "I've heard my daddy say that a million times."

"Well, you certainly don't have to be insulting. If you don't want the food…" She struggled to finish her sentence. "I guess I'll go tell Grandmother you refused her good intentions." She blinked repeatedly, reminding herself that she should hold her temper and she shouldn't ask him about his daddy or let on that she was aware his daddy was dead. "I won't tell her you were down right nasty about it." Katherine whirled around.

"Wait," James Everett called. "Don't offend Mrs. Carter. She's a nice lady. I'll take the food." He sheepishly wiped his hands down the front of his pants and reached out. "I didn't mean to sound ungrateful."

Katherine turned and gave him the sack.

He unrolled the top and looked inside. "Looks good." He smiled. "What's your name?'

"Mr. Dodie and Miss Odessa call me Little Missy but my real name is Katherine Elizabeth Langford." She stepped back, sat down on the row of bricks extending past the cellar door and carefully tucked her dress underneath her legs. "I like being called Little Missy," she mused, "You may call me Little Missy."

James Everett nodded. "I heard Mrs. Carter tell the preacher last Sunday that you and your mother would be coming for a visit. She said y'all would be moving to Shadow Springs if your daddy gets the president's job at the First State Bank."

"Yes, we're sure he's going to get the job just as soon as Mr. Tucker retires." Katherine smiled. "And we'll be moved and settled in long before school starts. I'll be enrolling in the seventh grade." She held her head up high. "I finished top of my class at Stockton Academy." For some reason Katherine felt the need to divulge that information. She hoped it wouldn't be perceived as bragging, but for some reason, and she wasn't sure why, she wanted to impress her new acquaintance. "What grade will you be in?" she asked.

"Seventh grade," he answered, closing the paper bag. "I'll be in Mrs. Dilbert's room. You too, but…." He stepped back and sized her up. "You sure are little for your age."

"Yes, I know. I'm petite like my mother," she replied, twisting her shoulders back and forth.

"Well." He grinned. "We only have one seventh grade teacher." He raised his eyebrows. "So you'll be in her room and…she's strict when it comes to reciting stuff, like The Gettysburg Address and The Declaration of Independence."

"I like reciting," Katherine responded, trying to decide if James Everett was purposely trying to be intimidating.

"Well, if you like that kind of stuff, you'll be all right." He glanced over his shoulder to see if Travis was finished with the unloading. "I don't care for it, but I've pretty much learned most of it anyway from hearing Travis, Jo Nell, and Sadie when they were learning it."

"Jo Nell and Sadie, are they your sisters?"

"Yeah, Travis is the oldest and then Jo Nell and Sadie, I'm next and then Curtis and Karen; they're twins. They ain't started to school yet. They're four."

"Wow, you have a large family." Katherine stood up. "You don't ever have to worry about being lonely, do you?"

"No." He shook his head. "Ain't got time to be lonely. There's too…"

"James Everett," Travis called from across the yard, interrupting their conversation. " Come on, we've got to go."

"I'm coming," he yelled back and then looked at Katherine. "Thank Mrs. Carter for me and tell her I'll thank her properly when I come back." He ran toward his brother.

Katherine followed him and watched as he climbed into the cab of the truck. Travis shook Mr. Dodie's hand and said, "I'll be back next week to get started on the well house roof."

"See ya den." Mr. Dodie waved as they drove away. "Dat's one fine young man," he said aloud. "He's hard working and polite too. He wants to go to Bible college, says the Lord has done called him to preach."

"Do all preachers have to go to Bible college?" Katherine asked.

"Don't have to," Mr. Dodie said, shaking his head. "Some preachers go to Bible college and some jest start preaching right off. I figure it's all in the way the Lord calls dem."

Katherine didn't fully understand what Mr. Dodie meant, but she didn't want him to know, so she nodded and walked back with him to the house.

Miss Odessa had run her mother and grandmother out of the kitchen and they were in the parlor looking through boxes of pictures. They spent the rest of the afternoon reminiscing about old times and mourning the fact that their visits had been limited because New York City and Chicago were so far away. Grandmother Kate lamented that even after her son-in-law had been promoted and transferred to Atlanta her husband's long illness with cancer had prevented travel. Their letters had kept them in touch, but had only served as a substitute for time spent together.

Katherine's mother openly wept as she spoke of the miscarriage that had kept her from attending her father's funeral and the emptiness she was still struggling with. "I think that's why Benton finally agreed to apply for the job here in Shadow Springs." She wiped her eyes. "He thinks being with family will ease the pain."

"Nothing can take away the pain of losing a child," Grandmother Kate sympathized. "I personally know that, but family can help you bear the burden."

Katherine sat quietly in the big armchair at the other end of the parlor. She dangled her feet and pondered the adult conversation she was sure she wasn't meant to overhear. She remembered her mother being in the hospital, but she had not known about a baby or the pain her mother was going through. Katherine's parents had never spoken to her about their problems, but she was not oblivious to the fact that her mother had become sad and distant, her father too. Things were adding up now; she was beginning to understand her father's sudden decision to move, his over-compensating for his lovely wife's mood changes and his desperate attempt to manipulate how people perceived him and his family. Public opinion had always been her father's number one priority. He felt his profession demanded that he live a life of virtue and respect. People had to trust him or they would not do business with his bank.

Katherine remained quiet. She listened and tried to sort out the details, but their words became whispers and her eyes became heavy. She fought sleep as long as she could, but finally she surrendered and when she woke up it was time to go home. She and her mother hugged everyone, said goodbye and started back down the hill. Her mother carried a big bag full of leftovers and Katherine carried the cat calendar that Grandmother Kate had taken down from above the mantel and had given to her as a take home gift. Her heart was full. She thanked God for Mr. Dodie and Miss Odessa and for the good food. She thanked Him for the beautiful cat calendar. But most of all, she thanked God for her grandmother and for her grandmother's house. It was a place where she felt welcomed and loved. She couldn't wait to start her new life there.

Chapter 3

Several long, apprehensive days went by before Katherine's daddy received confirmation that he would be taking over Mr. Tucker's job as the President at the First State Bank; however, Mr. Tucker thought it would be better if her daddy waited to accept his position until after the auditor was finished with his audit. He was convinced that his retirement should wait, too, just to make sure no minor details were overlooked. He was anxious to leave the banking world forever but he was willing to postpone the move to his newly purchased Texas ranch for a few weeks if necessary.

Benton Langford wasn't happy about the delay, but he had resigned himself to the fact that there wasn't anything he could do about it. The Board of Directors were so used to doing whatever Herschel Tucker told them to do that they didn't even bat an eye when he decided to postpone his exodus. Benton tried not to become resentful, but it did perturb him that the whim of one man could derail his well-planned-out future. Patience was not one of his virtues but being realistic was, so he and his wife decided to send Katherine ahead to live with her grandmother. They would remain behind and wait for the current bank president to decide when the passing of the torch would be appropriate. Katherine was absolutely overjoyed with their decision. She was in a hurry to settle in at her grandmother's house and find out what had happened to Wiley Holloway.

The mystery of his demise was haunting her relentlessly, but she knew she couldn't let her curiosity become a hindrance again, like it did when she decided to find out how the revolving doors worked at Yancey's Department Store. Instead of stepping out with her mother, Katherine continued to go around and around, focusing all of her attention on the center pole rather than being mindful of her dress tail. She was completely caught off guard when her skirt and petticoat bunched up in a wad and wedged in between the opening and one of the partitions, making it impossible for her to move. She was stuck, she couldn't budge, not even the tiniest little bit.

Her mother didn't notice she wasn't behind her and Katherine certainly didn't want to alert her, but desperation set in when angry shoppers began to line up on both sides of the doors and loudly complain about not being able to get in or out.

A tall, lean lady tapped on the glass, motioned for Katherine to push on the door while an older, plump, gray haired woman yelled her opinion of what type of punishment the unsupervised child should receive for causing such an inconvenience.

"That child should have a spanking," she yelled, with her hands on her hips. "Where is her mother?"

Katherine's mother was taken aback by the disturbance, but not nearly as much as when she discovered her daughter had caused it.

"I'm here!" she answered in a low voice, trying to remain calm. She wanted to defuse the angry crowd so she tried not to show her displeasure toward Katherine for not keeping up or show how concerned she was that her daughter was trapped in the glass revolving doors for the entire world to see. But she made no effort to hide her feelings toward the loudmouthed woman, who would not shut up. She kept yelling, "Where is her mother? Where is her mother?"

"I'm here," Elizabeth Langford answered, while tugging on the lady's arm. "Please be quiet, you are only making matters worse." She stepped forward and pried her fingers between the metal doors.

"How dare you tell me to be quiet!" the lady retaliated.

"Katherine, push," her mother ordered, in a half whisper, trying to ignore the tyrant behind her. "Push."

Tears filled Katherine's eyes. Panic rose from the pit of her stomach and Samson-like strength filled her arms. She pushed with all her might and the next thing she knew, the door burst open and completely ripped off the bottom half of her dress. She stepped out, naked from the waist down, except for her underwear.

Her mother was so embarrassed by her daughter's unintentional striptease that she proclaimed she would never step foot back into that department store. But her self-imposed boycott became such a hardship during the storewide sales event that she was forced to renege on her proclamation. Her weakness was justified however, by Katherine's oath to never do that again.

After that, Katherine promised herself that she would be more cautious and try to control her curious streak, but the unanswered questions of James Everett's daddy's death plagued her constantly. She knew it was going to be very difficult to keep herself in check once she made the move to Shadow Springs, but she was excited about her trip. She hardly slept a wink the night before.

Her mother would not allow her to ride the train alone, so they both boarded early the next morning. Elizabeth Anne planned to return to Atlanta later that same day but was going to take advantage of the three-hour delay between trains by treating everyone to lunch at the Grand Hotel. She and her husband had spent the first night of their honeymoon there fourteen years ago and she was excited about returning. She wanted her daughter to experience the luxury and grandeur of the magnificent landmark.

While they waited for Grandmother Kate and Mr. Dodie to meet them at the Hollinsville Train Station, Katherine studied her mother's light-hearted mood. She seemed more at ease, as if she had stepped out from under the cloud of sadness that had slowly and methodically overtaken her. Katherine didn't know the exact cause of her mother's sadness, only what she had overheard that day, and she was sure many details were being kept from her, but she hoped the worst was over. She hoped her daddy's new job and new surroundings would return her mother back to her old self. She liked the beautiful, smiling woman standing next to her.

The Grand Hotel was grand indeed. Its tall ceilings were covered with a mural of angels and puffy clouds and were sectioned off by gold trimmed beams in the shape of a huge umbrella. The thick, plush carpet and French provincial furniture filled the lobby with an ambiance of elegance fit for the very rich and well to do. Katherine was impressed with the craftsmanship and details of the design, but was disappointed with the over decorated dining room and the food offered on the menu. The small portions were beautifully presented on fine china, but they were tasteless and bland. The cook at the Grand Hotel wasn't nearly as good a cook as Miss Odessa and Katherine was tempted to voice her opinion, but she dared not say it aloud because she didn't want to upset her mother again. She had already earned a sharp disapproving stare from her earlier when she attempted to speak her mind when Mr. Dodie wasn't allowed inside the hotel.

"Colored folks must go to the back," the doorman had said, pointing toward the alley.

Mr. Dodie had lowered his eyes and nodded.

"But he's hungry too." Katherine had tried to reason with the doorman. She did not understand why Mr. Dodie couldn't eat lunch with them. She had wanted to request an explanation, but immediately decided to drop the subject because her mother had raised her eyebrows and had given her a look that told her it was in her best interest not to continue the conversation. Katherine knew she was skating on thin ice. Her behavior might not only upset her mother, but might embarrass Mr. Dodie, too.

"It's all right, little one," Mr. Dodie had said. "Don't you worry none, I take no offence."

After a long, leisurely and disappointing lunch, Mr. Dodie met them in the parking lot and drove them back to the station in time for Katherine's mother to catch her train, They waved goodbye from the platform and waited until the caboose was completely out of sight, then they hurriedly got back into the car and headed for Shadow Springs.

The sun had already set by the time they arrived at her grandmother's house. Mr. Dodie helped Katherine unload her suitcases and carry them upstairs.

"Dis here was your mother's old bedroom," he said, putting the bags down. "Missus Kate had me bring some thangs down from the attic. She wanted your room to look like it did when Miss Beff Anne was a little girl."

"Oh, it's beautiful!" Katherine whispered.

Mr. Dodie picked up the smallest bag and placed it on the bed. "Yes, indeed dis room is beautiful." He grinned. "And it's good to have you here to enjoy it." He took a deep breath. "You go on and get settled now. The morning will be here afore you know it." He backed out of the room and closed the door.

Katherine looked around. Pink ruffled curtains framed the large white canopy bed that stood in the middle of the room. The floral print on the wallpaper matched the bedspread and the skirt on the side table. A stepstool, almost hidden by the dust ruffle, stuck out near the top of the headboard and a dresser with an oversized mirror set against the wall on the other side of the bed. A glass tray with a brush, a comb and a small blue, heart-shaped bottle of perfume gave prominence to the top of the dresser and called attention to the jewelry box sitting next to it. Katherine walked over and opened the lid. A lovely ballerina popped up and twirled around and around, as if she were dancing to the music. The space above the chest-of-drawers had a large portrait of a little girl, about Katherine's age, dressed in a pink dress, trimmed with a gray satin ribbon. She was standing in a field of wild flowers and there were little, white, fluffy specks of dandelions dancing all around her. The picture was so mesmerizing Katherine could hardly take her eyes off of it.

"The bathroom is down the hall." Grandmother Kate poked her head inside.

Katherine jumped.

"I didn't mean to scare you."

"That's okay, I was trying to take all this in." She waved her arms. "This room makes me feel like a princess."

"Your mother used to say the same thing. She called it her castle."

"Castle, yes." Katherine nodded. "A beautiful castle."

Grandmother Kate smiled. "Are you tired?"

"Yes, ma'am," she answered. "I'm very tired."

"Well then, Katherine… I mean… Little Missy, go ahead and get ready for bed. You can put the rest of your things away tomorrow."

Katherine unzipped the small suitcase and took out her pajamas and the cat calendar. She looked up and grinned. "Little Missy. You remembered my new name."

"Of course, I remembered." Her grandmother blew her a kiss and closed the bedroom door.

Little Missy was awakened early the next morning by the loud conversation going on beneath her bedroom window. She jumped out of bed and ran to the double windows and flung them open. She saw Miss Odessa standing on the side porch, waiting for her husband to walk down the steps.

"Be sure to check under the old speckled hen. I think she's trying to set again." She leaned over the porch railing and handed Mr. Dodie the egg-gathering basket. "Don't gather all the eggs cause I think we should let dat be Little Missy's job. She'll problee want to earn a little spending money."

"I speck so, Odessa," he answered, nodding his head. "It's a good thang to learn early bout making your own way."

"Dats the way I figured it too." His wife chuckled and wiped her hands on her apron and then walked back inside.

Little Missy waited until Mr. Dodie made it down the trail to the henhouse then she darted out into the hall and toward the bathroom. The smell of bacon frying encouraged her to speed through the process of getting dressed. At home, her mother wouldn't allow her to go to the breakfast table without being fully dressed, hair combed and teeth brushed. It didn't make sense to her to brush her teeth before breakfast and then brush them again after she finished eating, but her mother insisted that was a required regiment for all civilized young ladies. She thought it was perplexing nonsense but she never objected because she knew it would do her no good.

She was in such a hurry to get downstairs it didn't occur to her that she should knock on the bathroom door before entering, but the minute she saw a half-naked, bald man standing in front of the mirror, smearing shaving cream on his face, she realized that not only should she have knocked, but she should have listened, too.

"I...I...I'm sorry, sir." Her mouth gaped open. "I didn't know..."

The startled gentleman grabbed his robe and covered his front part, still exposing the backside of his blue, striped boxer underwear. "No harm done," he stammered. "I'll finish up as quickly as possible."

"No need to hurry." She slammed the door, turned around and accidentally ran into her grandmother. "I...I," she stuttered. "There's a man..."

"I know." Grandmother Kate held her by her shoulders. "I forgot to tell you about Mr. Boggs, our boarder."

"Oh, I didn't know you took in boarders," she gasped, trying to erase from her mind the image of the skinny, middle aged, shirtless man wearing striped underwear and socks held up by sock supports.

"It's okay, really," Grandmother Kate assured. "Mr. Boggs will recover and so will you. No need to fret. It's all done and over and nobody is the worse for it." Grandmother Kate brushed her hand across Little Missy's cheek. "Now, put a smile on your face. You can use the downstairs bathroom next to the parlor."

Little Missy no longer wanted to hurriedly get dressed. She made her way downstairs and slowly washed her face, brushed her teeth and combed her hair, dragging the process out as long as possible. She didn't relish the thought of sitting across the breakfast table from the man she had met under such embarrassing circumstances. It terrified her to think that she was going to have to face him every morning.

When she finally finished, she inched her way back to her room, got dressed and sat on the edge of her bed, waiting a full fifteen minutes before entering the kitchen.

Miss Odessa was gathering the dirty dishes. She heard the floor creak and looked up. "I was bout to send the cavalry after you." She frowned. "Ain't you hungry, child?"

"Yes, ma'am, I'm starved." Little Missy quickly squeezed into the nearest chair. "But I was waiting for the boarder to leave. I..."

"Yeah, I heard bout the bathroom encounter. Mr. Boggs mumbled something bout it as he gulped down his breakfast." Miss Odessa pushed the dishes aside. "Neville is such a timid fellow, usually don't speak unless he's spoken to, but dis morning he went on and on bout the unfortunate incident."

"Oh, was he upset?" Little Missy blushed.

"Sho was, especially after I told him you'd problee have nightmares for the rest of your life." Miss Odessa laughed a near-deafening laugh and clapped her hands together. "I told him I'd problee have nightmares, too, if I'd seen such a sight." She rolled her eyes. "His face turned white as a field of cotton and he rushed out of here faster than a spring-loaded steal trap."

"Miss Odessa, why did you say such a thing?"

"Cause he's so tight lipped and guarded. His job as auditor has robbed him of a personality. He's been coming here for the last seven years to audit the bank's books; you'd think he'd be friendly. Usually stays bout a week; dats plenty of time to get to know folks, but he don't even make an effort. Most time we don't even know he's here cause he never leaves his room unless it's to eat or go to work…or go to the bathroom." Miss Odessa pressed her lips together, trying to stifle a smile. "I ain't never seen him act like he did dis morning, almost comical."

"Well, I don't blame him for being upset. I'm upset too. I didn't mean to walk in on him like that. I don't know how I'll ever face him."

"You'll sit down, smile and say good morning to him, dats how you'll face him." She leaned over the table. "You'll show him you're not gonna make a big deal over it. Dat way he'll know he needs to stop being so gloomy all the time and learn dat life is too short to worry bout things dat cannot be changed."

Little Missy's mind drifted back to the revolving door incident. She certainly wanted to put that episode behind her, never to speak about it again. "I think you're right," she agreed. "I should try to pretend I didn't see what I saw."

"Dats the spirit," Miss Odessa encouraged. "Now, let's get you fed."

The breakfast menu at Grandmother Kate's house was certainly different from what Little Missy was used to. There wasn't a poached egg, a glass of orange juice or dry toast anywhere on the table, instead there were two big plates of fried eggs and bacon, a very large bowl of grits and a platter of cathead biscuits and sausage gravy, a stack of flapjacks, a dish of butter, a jar of syrup and three different kinds of homemade jellies for her to choose from.

"Do you cook like this every day?" she asked, picking up her fork.

"Sho do," Miss Odessa answered. "I believe in starting the day off with a good hardy breakfast. We need our strength around here, farming is hard work." She raised her eyebrows and looked over her shoulder. "You need to go ahead and eat afore the day laborers get here. Dey done been working two hours on an empty stomach. Dodie will be bringing dem in any minute." She pointed toward the clock standing in the corner of the dining room. "See dat big hand? When it points straight up it will be seven o'clock; chow time for the hired hands." Miss Odessa laughed softly. "You best help your plate and move on into the kitchen cause there ain't gonna be nothing left once dey get in here."

Little Missy quickly placed two pieces of bacon and a biscuit on her plate. She scooted back from the table and headed for the other room.

"Whoa, whoa." Miss Odessa stopped her. "It's gonna be a long time till high noon. You gonna need more than dat to hold you over." She plopped an egg and a helping of grits on her plate. "Now, dats better," she said, giving her a nod of approval. "You'll thank me later."

Little Missy barely had time to sit down at the kitchen table before the screen door burst open. Mr. Dodie and three big black men rushed passed her. He nodded to her as he walked by. "Odessa has a list of chores for you to do. We figured you'd want to earn your keep and a little spending money, too." He winked. "The Good Book speaks against idle hands."

"Idle hands, earning my keep, what do you mean?" She spoke the words but nobody was there to hear them. Mr. Dodie had already stepped into the dining room and had pulled the pocket-doors closed. "Oh my," she whispered.

Chapter 4

The noise from the dining room died down once everybody was served. There was no time to carry on a conversation. Finishing breakfast and getting back to the fields before the temperatures became unbearable was the major concern but Little Missy didn't understand that. She had no concept of the hardships of farm life or how much time and effort was involved until Grandmother Kate slid the handwritten list in front of her.

"Odessa and I tried to remember all the things your mother used to do," she said, sitting down beside her. "Elizabeth Anne took pride in earning money for new school clothes each summer." She pointed to the list. "But I think we may have to adjust the amount you get paid, times have changed a little."

"Oh, my parents will buy my school clothes. You don't have to pay me Grandmother. I don't mind earning my keep but…I'm not sure I know how."

"Don't worry, I've asked James Everett to help you. He's going to teach you how to do all the things on this list. After that," she winked, "you'll be able to speed through your chores and wonder how you'll occupy the rest of your time."

Little Missy pushed her unfinished breakfast aside. "There are certainly a lot of items on the list." She frowned. "How do I…?"

James Everett lightly knocked on the screen door, opened it and stepped inside. "Mrs. Carter," he called.

"Good morning." Grandmother Kate looked up and smiled. "You want something to eat?"

"No ma'am, I've already had breakfast." He nodded to Little Missy. "You ready to get started? I promised Travis I'd help him with the roof as soon as we get finished. The rain has put us way behind."

"I guess." She pushed back from the table. "How do I change out chicken watering jars?" she asked, holding up the list.

James Everett shook his head. "Come on." He drew a deep breath. "I'll show you."

Little Missy followed him down the path to the chicken coop, careful not to veer off onto the dew-covered grass. She didn't want to get her shoes wet but she dared not mention it because it was obvious her teacher would not be concerned about such a minor thing. His bare feet were crusted with calluses and dirt. She reasoned a little dew would not bother him at all.

James Everett stopped at the hand pump and filled the empty bucket before entering the coop. "You'll need to wash the jars once a week, but you have to check the water every day." He lifted the door latch, stepped inside and waited for her to join him. "Make sure you always shut the door, don't want the chickens to get out, but more important, don't want varmints getting in."

"What kind of varmints?"

"Foxes, weasels, possums or egg sucking dogs." He sighed. "Lots of different varmints, maybe a bobcat or…"

"Stop," she interrupted. "You're kidding, right?"

"Nope, ain't got time to kid around." James Everett picked up the first quart jar, turned it right side up and unscrewed the lid. "This one needs water." He quickly filled the jar, screwed the lid back on and flipped it upside down, making sure the ring filled with water. "That's all there is to it…understand?" He didn't wait for her to answer instead; he walked to the next jar. "What you waiting on?" he asked.

"Oh, nothing," she answered, wondering why he was in such a hurry. It seemed to her that he could be a little more patient considering she had never seen a chicken watering jar before.

By ten o'clock he had sharply, hurriedly and impatiently given her instructions on all the items on the list. He'd showed her how to feed the chickens, gather the eggs, water the herb garden and pick beans. "You can snap them later, but I ain't gonna hang around to help. I promised to help Travis and I aim to keep my promise. We've got bills to pay."

"Well, by all means, go…go now." Little Missy pushed her brown hair away from her face and rebelliously grabbed the basket of beans from his hand. "I don't need you to help me snag the beans. I'm perfectly capable of snagging them by myself."

"Oh Lord, don't tell me you have never snapped beans before."

"What do you mean?"

"I mean you snap beans not snag them…don't you know anything?"

"I know you're rude and I know there is no cause for it. This is the first time I've lived on a farm. I bet if you lived where I've lived, New York, Chicago and Atlanta, you wouldn't know what to do," she smirked. "I bet you'd get lost the first day."

"Maybe so," James Everett bantered back. "But this is Alabama and I ain't lost and I know how to snap beans." He shook his head and stomped off.

"Rude," she yelled, as she watched him make his way across the field. He had pushed her to her limit, making her feel inferior. He wouldn't let her ask any questions and he acted as if he knew everything. Her temper simmered just thinking about his smart aleck ways.

Miss Odessa sat on the back porch swing and waited until Little Missy made it back to the house. "I was bout to go looking for you. James Everett speeded past me like I was the turtle and he was the hare." She patted the cushion next to her. "Come sit a spell and tell me why he was in such a hurry?"

"I don't know." Little Missy climbed the steps, opened the screen door and set the basket on the small wicker table. She slumped down in the oversized chair facing Miss Odessa and said, "I've eaten green beans a million times, wonder why the cook never mentioned anything about snapping beans?"

"Maybe she figured snapping beans was her job or maybe she figured rich folks wouldn't snap beans even if dey knew how."

"Do you think I'm rich, Miss Odessa?"

"I think most folks would consider you rich."

"Is being rich a bad thing?"

"No, not as long as you don't let your money rule you." Miss Odessa leaned forward. "It don't matter how much money you have, it's what you do with your money dat makes you rich. Love for the Lord and love for family is what truly makes a person rich." She raised both hands and rocked her head from side to side. "Child, you're looking at a rich woman." She laughed out loud. "I'm rich with blessings."

"Me too, I'm rich with blessings." Little Missy sat up straight. "But I don't know how to snap beans. Will you teach me?"

"I sho will if you'll tell me what's got James Everett in such a whirlwind."

"I don't know, Miss Odessa, I swear I don't know. The first time I met him he was nice enough, but this morning he was down right rude. He acted as if he was running a race, rushing to finish with me so he could help his brother with the well house roof." She searched for the right words. "I have no idea what turned him into such a… dill pickle…unless maybe he's worried about having bills to pay…he mentioned that once or twice."

"Problee so." Miss Odessa used the bottom half of her apron as a fan. "Dey were barely scraping by when Wiley was alive but now…I'm sure it's much more difficult for dem. Poor Mary Ruth has started taking in ironing and keeping house for Judge Wilkes and his persnickety wife." She stopped fanning and raised her right hand. "I swear Charlotte Wilkes is the prime example of a demanding fiend." She squinted her eyes. "Evil in the way she always wants everything to be just so so…perfect beyond perfect." She shook her head. "Problee working Mary Ruth to the bone with all dem parties and fancy luncheons she's always giving. Yes indeed, the Holloway family is going through some trying times."

"I know I'm not supposed to ask and I know Mother wouldn't be pleased, but I've been wondering…how did Mr. Holloway die?"

"Well, you're bound to find out one way or another, might as well be from me rather than from the gossips in town." She looked around, making sure James Everett was nowhere in sight. "It looks like…most folks think," she hesitated, "Wiley shot himself…but dat don't make sense to me. He'd been off the whiskey for months and was working for Mr. Tucker."

"Mr. Tucker, the bank president? He was working at the bank?"

"No honey, not at the bank…on Mr. Tucker's cattle farm. Wiley didn't know nothing bout banking but he was a good ranch hand… when he was sober…anyway, like I was saying, Wiley had turned his life around." Miss Odessa started fanning again. "It's a shame, dat's what it is, a pure shame dat James Everett had to find his daddy dead, laying a corpse out behind Mr. Tucker's barn."

"James Everett found him?"

"He sho did. It seems dat Mary Ruth got worried cause it was way past time for Wiley to get home from work. She problee feared he had fell off the wagon, dat he was laid up drunk somewhere so she sent James Everett to look for his daddy. I'm sure it never occurred to her dat her son would make such a discovery, dat he'd find the gun in his daddy's hand."

"Oh, how awful."

"Sho was. The sheriff said James Everett walked into the police station, hands covered with blood and a blank stare on his face. It took a long time afore he was able to speak and den it was only a whisper. He whispered his daddy's name and told dem where to find him and nothing more…not another word." Miss Odessa blinked back the tears. "Poor boy." She wiped underneath her eyes with the corner of her apron. "Ain't no words to describe the heartache he must be suffering."

Little Missy twisted the hem of her cotton skirt into a tight knot. She knew her mother would frown at her intentionally creating wrinkles but it was her way to alleviate stress. Her curiosity had been satisfied, she now knew how Wiley Holloway had died, but the reality of such an unexpected revelation was unsettling. "Why did he do it?" she asked. "Why would he leave his family with such a hardship?"

"Dats what I don't understand. It jest don't make sense." Miss Odessa shook her head and bit her lower lip. "We may never know why he did what he did. The Bible speaks about secret things belonging to the Lord."

"Are you saying God is going to keep this a secret?" Little Missy asked, leaning forward. Her eyes widened.

"No, no. I'm not saying dat." Miss Odessa spoke softly. "I'm saying dat God knows more than we do and it's up to Him to reveal things to us…a little at a time, or not at all…it's His decision." She leaned forward too and whispered. "He don't spect us to understand why things are the way dey are. Dat would be too paramount for us to figure out." Miss Odessa straightened her posture. "We don't have to have the wisdom of Solomon to know we have a higher power taking care of us."

Chapter 5

The days went by quickly. Little Missy had been at her grandmother's house almost two weeks and had finished her internship with James Everett. Somehow she had managed to grasp the concept of how to accomplish her daily chores from his brief schooling and had settled into a routine. Mr. Boggs had finally vacated his rented room, after extending his stay by one full week and two days. His leaving relieved Little Missy of her forced pleasantries and her dread of trying to make polite conversation with him at breakfast each morning. It didn't matter how many times she asked about his health or if he thought it might rain and cool things off, his response was the same, a half-hardy grunt or a nod. Although the Carter household perceived his departure as a welcomed relief it only served as a springboard for multiple speculations from the community busybodies as to why he had extended his stay far beyond normal.

Katherine Carter had wasted no time in cleaning, dusting and making his room ready for her daughter and son-in-law when, and if, Herschel Tucker ever decided to retire. Benton and Elizabeth Anne were anxious to make the transition and their anxieties were becoming more and more apparent with each passing day. Little Missy had not been privy to every conversation between her grandmother and her mother but she had noticed the long distance phone calls had become more frequent and seemingly more stress laden. The last one more so than the others because she had overheard Grandmother Kate tell her mother not to cry on more than one occasion. Little Missy didn't like being kept in the dark. She needed stability. She needed assurance that her new life wasn't going to be taken away from her.

Living in Shadow Springs was different from anything Little

Missy had ever known. She no longer felt the loneliness and boredom of being an only child, living in the confines of the city, swallowed up by the demands and pressures of being the perfect offspring of perfect parents. But the uncertainty about her father's job made her feel like a lost puppy. She waited until Miss Odessa was finished with her scripture reading time before she joined her on the back porch the next morning.

"Are you finished?" she asked, softly. "I can come back."

"No, child." Miss Odessa closed her Bible and laid it on the swing next to her. "I'm finished. Do you need something?"

"I need...I was wondering." Her voice trailed off. She didn't know how to approach the subject. "I don't want to interrupt your scripture time. You said time spent with the Lord is..." She stared at her feet. "Is..."

"Time spent with the Lord is a daily necessity, as necessary as breathing." Miss Odessa finished her sentence.

"Yes, as necessary as breathing," she repeated. Her small hands began to shake. "Do you know...?" She cleared her throat; trying to summon the courage to ask the questions she was desperate to know the answers to... when will Father start his job? When will my parents move here? She formed the words in her mind and was about to speak them, but her grandmother called from inside the kitchen.

"Yoo-hoo, where is everybody?"

"We're out here," Miss Odessa responded. "We're on the back porch."

"Good." Mrs. Carter walked through the doorway, waving her purse and white gloves. "I've been on the phone with Ivy Holcomb. She's Herschel Tucker's secretary and she knows him better than anybody. She seems to think he may not retire after all. She said he's acting like a spoiled child that doesn't want to play with his toys, but doesn't want anybody else to play with them either." She smoothed her hair and motioned toward her granddaughter. "Come on, you and I are going into town to do a little shopping and...I need to stop by the bank."

Miss Odessa shot up unusually fast, causing the swing to sway in every direction. "Now, don't go getting all upset. Mrs. Holcomb loves to tote tales. I've known her to stretch the truth many times and so have you."

"Yes, Odessa, that's true but it's high time Herschel moves on. Benton and Elizabeth Anne have sold their home in Atlanta…it isn't fair for them to be homeless and jobless too, I might add, just because Herschel is having second thoughts about retiring."

"Grandmother," Little Missy sighed.

Realizing her actions were unbecoming of her Southern upbringing and upsetting to her granddaughter, Mrs. Carter stopped abruptly and said, "Oh, sugar, I don't know what came over me. I shouldn't be carrying on like this." She calmed her voice. "I may be overreacting and a bit impatient." She turned to Odessa. "You're right, I don't have all the facts." She suffocated her annoyances and quickly attempted to revive her normal cheerful personality. "I'll just stop by the bank, withdraw a little shopping money and ask to speak with the outgoing president so I can wish him well and politely inquire about his immediate plans." She drew in a deep breath and moistened her lips. Her face relaxed. "Honey attracts more bees than vinegar. Don't you agree?"

"Yesss," Miss Odessa answered suspiciously. "I certainly agree, but your visit might be interpreted as a nosy mother-in-law on a fact-finding mission."

"Well, that would be a true assessment, indeed it would." Katherine Carter rubbed her bare arm, as if to ward off the chill of the conversation and then she cleared her throat. "Come on Little Missy, we have a mission to accomplish."

After a quick trip to the bathroom to wash her face and hands, a few brush strokes through her slightly tangled hair and a nod of approval from her grandmother, Little Missy found herself in the front seat of the car and on her way into town.

The square was surrounded by simple storefronts and small, no-frills businesses, reminding her of a picture of an old-fashioned town she had seen in one of her library books.

"Oh," she whispered, pressing her face against the window. "Small, no tall building with elevators or revolving doors."

"Yes, our town is small and simple but we have everything we need," her grandmother answered, as she pulled into a parking space in front of the bank. "Over there," she pointed, "past the hardware store is the Piggly Wiggly, the Post Office and Dr. Whatley's clinic. And over yonder," she changed directions to the other side of the street, "is Nadine's Clothing Shop, the movie theater and the drug store." She put the car into park and switched off the engine. "Down the street, across from Cecil's Café is the mill. I hope we have time to check in with Grady before we leave."

"Grady who?"

"Grady Dewberry. He's been running the mill for me since before your grandfather died."

"What mill?"

"Carter's Mill. It's a cotton mill; we spin cotton into thread. Thomas and I ran it together until he got sick. I tried to run the mill and take care of him too but it finally became too much for me. I decided time with my dying husband was more important, so I asked Grady to take over." She cracked her window, opened the car door and lifted her purse from the floorboard. "He's your mother's old sweetheart." She quickly checked her reflection in the rearview mirror, turning her face from side to side; making sure her hastily applied lipstick wasn't smeared.

Little Missy watched her from a sideways glance, remembering the many times she had seen her mother do the same thing, but her mother didn't do a brief check, no, it was much more than that. Her routine was to painstakingly search for flaws, flaws she did not have. She had no imperfections, except her tendency to see them where they did not exist.

"Mother's old sweetheart?" A hint of surprise filled Little Missy's voice. It never occurred to her that her mother could have been attracted to any man other than her father.

"Yes, but that was years ago, when they were in high school." Grandmother Kate wiped the corners of her mouth with her little finger. "Good enough," she said, pressing her lips together. "Life is too short to worry about every little thing." She winked. "As long as I don't look like a clown or have lipstick on my teeth—that's good enough."

"I've never heard my mother say that. She thinks she needs to improve and she's constantly stressing about things."

"I've noticed, but when she was little, she was carefree and haphazard. I always had to remind her of something or the other, but..." Grandmother Kate sank back into the seat and stared straight ahead, as if she was looking at something far, far away, "Elizabeth Anne was such a happy child, until the tragic accident." A troubled look creased her face. "Loosing Tommy was hard on all of us, but...I thought she had gotten over..." Her words were barely audible. "I thought..."

Little Missy clutched the door handle but didn't attempt to get out of the car. Her thoughts quickly went back to the happy times when her home was filled with laughter, from both her parents. It was as if she woke up one day and everything was different. Her father was stiff and restrained, her mother was overcome by sadness and insecurity and there was an unspoken creed that she was to accept the situation with no questions asked.

"Grandmother." Her words snapped her grandmother out of her trance. "Mother used to laugh all the time, but she..." her voice wavered. "Do you think it is something I caused? Is it my fault?" She dropped her head.

"Oh, honey, no." Grandmother Kate reached over and lifted her chin.

"Absolutely not. Grownup things happen to grownups. What your parents are going through has nothing to do with you." She frowned. "You put that thought out of your mind. Okay?" She forced a smile. "You and I came to town to do some shopping, now, didn't we?"

Little Missy fought to hold back the tears. She breathed deeply, trying to pull herself together. "And we came here on a fact finding mission," she added.

"That we did." Her grandmother squeezed her arm. "Are you ready?"

"Yes, ma'am." She nodded.

The high ceilings and fan-swirled air inside the bank were a welcomed relief from the outside hot summer sun and sticky humidity. Mrs. Carter and her granddaughter stood in the middle of the lobby for a few seconds in order to regain their composure and to allow the tiny beads of perspiration to evaporate from across their foreheads.

"Mrs. Carter, what can I do for you today?" Darby Brooks, the head teller, called out from behind the counter. She batted her eyes and smiled as if she were presenting herself to a row of beauty queen judges. She had reluctantly come to work at the bank two years ago under the assumption that her teller job was a temporary one, just until something better came along. She was intelligent and quick-witted and capable of being a star employee but every now and then, she'd show her discontentment by letting it slip that she was more than ready for advancement to a higher paying job with more prestige. Her goal was to replace Ivy Holcomb as the secretary to the bank's president.

"Sure is hot out today, isn't it?" She fluffed her bleached blond hair and then slid her hands down to her tiny waist. "What brings you into town in the middle of the week?"

"Shopping, we're going to Nadine's," Grandmother Kate said, pushing Little Missy forward. "This is my granddaughter and she is in need of a wardrobe more suitable for farm living."

"Oh, that's right." Darby's forced smile exaggerated her thin lips; almost making them appear as if they had been hand-drawn across her face. "I've heard all about your daughter and her family moving here."

"I'm sure you have." Mrs. Carter restrained her voice, making sure not to show her irritation. She didn't like her family being the center of gossip and speculation. She pushed her withdrawal slip across the counter. "I need to withdraw a little spending money and," she looked toward the president's office, "I thought I might pay Hershel a visit while I'm here. Is he busy?"

"I'm not sure." Darby answered, opening her cash drawer.

From across the room, Little Missy had been under the misconception that Darby Brooks was very attractive, but upon a closer inspection many imperfections became obvious. Her dark eyes, very short lashes and barely visible cheekbones had been over-embellished to the point of making her look fake, like a department store mannequin. Little Missy's thoughts now were that she could certainly benefit from a few lessons from her mother.

Darby's voice displayed a hint of indifference as she counted out the money. Her attention was divided, focusing more on the president's office than on her customer. "Mr. Tucker is a busy man." She closed the drawer and glanced at her watch. "He may not be able to fit you in today. Maybe you should make an appointment."

"An appointment has never been necessary before. Hershel has always been available to me…my late husband was on the board of directors." Mrs. Carter stiffened. "You are aware of that, aren't you?"

"Yes, I am aware of that…I only meant …I thought you wanted to pay a friendly visit. I didn't know you were here on official business."

"It is a friendly visit," Katherine Carter answered, impatiently. "I won't keep him long." She placed her wallet inside her purse and stepped away from the counter. "You may tell him that…tell him I only need a few moments of his time."

"No need to deliver the message, Darby." Hershel Tucker came out of his office. He stood in the doorway and gave the teller a look of displeasure, letting her know that she had overstepped her duties. She met his gaze with a look of defiance, and then sharply turned her head.

After a moment of awkwardness, Hershel recovered enough to turn his attention back to Mrs. Carter. "Kate, I thought that was your voice." He waved her over. "You know you're always welcome…what can I do for you?"

"Not what you can do for me Hershel, but what I can do for you?" Katherine Carter strolled across the hallway with Little Missy in tow. "I was hoping you would allow me to host your retirement party."

"A party?" Little Missy whispered, tugging at her grandmother's arm.

"Shhh." Mrs. Carter muttered under her breath. "Hershel," she raised her voice and smiled, "you know I'm always looking for an excuse to outdo Charlotte Wilkes, we can't let her give all the parties."

He led the way past his secretary's empty desk. "Ivy's gone to the post office," he explained, while motioning them forward. "Come on in and have a seat."

The smell of leather and men's aftershave engulfed them as they entered the large, richly decorated office. Little Missy's first impression was that it was far superior to any office her daddy had ever occupied. She looked around; there was so much to see…an oversized portrait of a sprawling cattle ranch and a mount of a Texas longhorn was prominently displayed above his fine hand-carved mahogany desk and regal high-back leather chair. A floor to ceiling display case full of trophies, plaques and awards, celebrating Hershel Tucker's cattle farming abilities interrupted the imported wooden panels covering the walls.

The young girl stood in awe, not realizing she was calling attention to herself by standing while the others were seated.

"A-hem." Her grandmother cleared her throat. "Sweetie."

Little Missy jerked to attention and quickly sat down. She lowered her eyes, trying to hide her embarrassment.

Mr. Tucker paused. "I'm…not sure about a retirement party." He scratched his head. "I hadn't planned to make a big deal about my leaving."

"Oh, Hershel, surely you want to celebrate your many years of dedicated service." Mrs. Carter struggled to sound sincere. "It wouldn't be right to just quietly walk away without some type of celebration."

"Well, I don't know…" Mr. Tucker looked uncomfortable. "The audit is barely over, I'm still trying to make sure…uh…I mean…I really haven't had time to make any special plans."

"Don't you worry about the plans…I'll handle the planning, all you have to do is give me a date." Katherine Carter scooted to the edge of her chair. "I can pull things together in no time at all." She took a pen and small writing pad from her pocketbook. "Now, when will you be leaving?"

"Uh, maybe by the end of the month…I need to call your son-in-law and the board members and…"

"Fine, we'll wait while you make those calls." Mrs. Carter smiled. "No sense in putting things off. The sooner we get started the better." She motioned toward his phone. "Go ahead, don't mind us." She looked at her granddaughter and whispered loudly, "I'm so excited, aren't you?"

Little Missy wasn't sure how to answer, or even if she should answer. She now understood that the retirement party was only a ploy by her grandmother to accomplish her fact-finding mission, and a good ploy indeed, for it seemed to be working beautifully.

Chapter 6

Ivy Holcomb shifted the mail to her left hand and hurried toward Katherine Carter and her granddaughter. They had just stepped out of the bank and were about to descend the steps.

"Kate, is something wrong?" Ivy asked reluctantly. "Did our conversation this morning bring about a show down?" She placed her hand on her chest and struggled to catch her breath. She was slightly overweight, bigger on the bottom than the top. She wasn't used to running or sprinting up steps.

"Of course not," Katherine Carter replied, purposely waving the writing pad in front of her friend's face. "Hershel and I have been planning his retirement party."

"You what?" Ivy's face turned white, matching her hair color. She stared in disbelief.

"You heard me, we've been planning his retirement party."

"So he is going to retire…when? How did you get this information?" Ivy shaded her eyes and motioned for the others to back up under the shade of the porch. "He's been in such a conundrum lately, I honestly didn't think he was going to leave."

"Well, he is." Mrs. Carter's voice was giddy. She was elated to the point of sounding like a silly schoolgirl recounting the details of her prom date. "He'll be leaving before the end of the month and he called Benton and told him to be prepared to start his job immediately. He said he would help him get settled and then he's off to Texas."

"Kate, you are amazing. I don't know how you did it but," Ivy shook her head, "somehow you have managed to force his hand."

"It's a skill I learned from Thomas." Mrs. Carter beamed with pride. "Before he got sick he kept Hershel in line, he held him accountable."

"Yes, but now the directors let him walk all over them. They're like water running through a sieve. They don't even look at the reports." Ivy leaned closer and whispered. "Neville Boggs never had any questions when your husband served on the board, his audits were quick and easy. But he moved at a snail's pace with this last one. Hershel was constantly looking over his shoulders, pressuring him to finish. The more pressure Hershel applied the slower Neville got."

"I know, I thought he would never leave." Katherine Carter answered, glancing at her watch. "Oh my, look at the time." She placed her hands on Little Missy's shoulders. "I would love to stay and talk but we are pressed for time. This is Elizabeth Anne's daughter."

Mrs. Holcomb lowered her gaze. "I can see the resemblance. You're very pretty, just like your mother."

"Thank you," Little Missy said shyly. "Grandmother Kate and I are going shopping and then we're going to the mill."

Ivy Holcomb's eyebrows lifted sharply and a bemused expression crept across her face. She shifted her stance and turned back to her friend. "How does Grady feel about Elizabeth Anne moving back to Shadow Springs? Does he know?"

"I'm sure he does. The word has been out about Benton's new job for a while. He has surely been told multiple times by now." Mrs. Carter answered, with a hint of irritation in her voice. "But if he doesn't know, I will certainly enlighten him."

Little Missy pulled away from her grandmother and quickly made her way to the car. The name Grady Dewberry had already been spoken that morning and she didn't like what she'd heard. She wasn't anxious to meet him nor did she care what he thought. As a matter of fact, it was curious to her why his feelings would be an issue. Her mother and father would be moving here regardless of how he felt. It was her opinion that he was an employee of her grandmother's and nothing more. His feelings were of no interest to her.

She folded her arms and leaned against the car. "Maybe he's fat," she said aloud. "Maybe he's bald and wrinkled and…"

"If you're talking about Grady, you're wrong." Grandmother Kate interrupted. She crossed her arms and leaned against the car next to her granddaughter. "He is as handsome as ever but…" she hesitated, "if you're worried about he and Elizabeth Anne, you have no cause. Your mother made her choice years ago. She fell in love with your father when she was in college and that hasn't changed."

"Well, why did Mrs. Holcomb say what she said? I saw the look on her face."

"Ivy likes to talk. She likes to create drama, but the reality is your mother broke Grady's heart when she told him she was getting married. He moped around for months, hoping Elizabeth Anne would change her mind, but when she didn't, he refused to attend her wedding. He boasted that he would take no part in her mistake, but then he showed up at the reception drunk as a skunk, and declared that he would love her until the day he died." Mrs. Carter smiled. "But that was a long time ago and many things have changed since then."

"Did he ever marry?" Little Missy's spirits were hopeful.

"No," Grandmother Kate said, thoughtfully. "He met a young lady while he was in the army. He wrote home about her, told his mother he liked her a lot, but then I guess the romance fizzled. He stopped writing about her."

"Do you think he still has feelings for Mother?" Little Missy asked.

"Probably," Grandmother Kate answered, unfolding her arms. "It takes a long time to get over the heartbreak of your first love. He may still have feelings for your mother, but I don't think he is in love with her. I'm sure he has accepted that she doesn't love him."

"What about you, Grandmother, how do you feel?" Little Missy was resentful; she felt loyalty toward the father. She didn't want to seem disrespectful but it bothered her that Grandmother Kate defended her mother's old beau. "Are you sorry Mr. Dewberry and Mother's relationship didn't work out?"

"No, I'm not sorry. I like Grady, but I love my daughter and I want her to be happy. She loves your father and he loves her."

"But Mother doesn't seem happy…I'm afraid."

"What are you afraid of?"

"I'm not sure. I don't know."

"You don't have to be afraid of Grady." Grandmother Kate lowered her voice, almost to a whisper. "Would you rather we put off visiting the mill?"

"Yes, please."

Nadine made a big fuss over how much Little Missy resembled her mother. "It's like stepping back in time," she said, twirling the young girl around so she could determine her size. "I've got exactly what you need."

She led her customers to the back wall and then she began to hastily jerk items of clothing off the racks. She shoved them toward Grandmother Kate, hesitating long enough to get a yes or no nod and then she either put them back or draped them across her arm. Within a few seconds she had amassed an armload of outfits and was leading the way down the hall. Little Missy was slightly bothered that neither lady consulted her about her likes or dislikes. She thought about trying to voice her opinion, but found no opportunity so she simply stood blank-faced and speechless.

Nadine stopped at the dressing room, counted the garments, making sure she had the same amount of tops as bottoms and then she immersed herself into what seemed to be a one-sided conversation. She rambled on about how fast time rushes by, how her life was like a freight train running downhill and how difficult it was for her to keep up with all the happenings going on around her. She expressed her delight that the Carter family was finally going to be reunited and reiterated how she'd always felt it was a mistake for Elizabeth Anne to move off up north with all those Yankees.

Her constant babble and high-pitched continuous chatter were a distraction for Little Missy. She wondered how on earth her grandmother was able to make sense of the tall, redheaded, middle-aged woman's conversation. It seemed her hodgepodge of thoughts were being spoken aloud, but not to anyone in particular and with no expectations of anyone responding.

The whole ordeal was confusing, but not unsuccessful. Little Missy and her grandmother left the store with two large shopping bags. She was so excited when she got home she didn't carry her new things upstairs. She wanted to show them to Miss Odessa so she rushed from room to room shouting her name.

"Is the house on fire?" Miss Odessa called from the dining room. "I swear, I ain't heard the likes of such carrying on since Jasper Easterwood caught hisself with a fish hook." She listened as the sound of footsteps circled from the hall to the kitchen. "Stay where you are, I'm coming." Miss Odessa stopped polishing the silver tray and waddled into the kitchen. She pulled out a chair and waited while Little Missy dumped the contents of the bags on the table.

"Did you leave anything in the sto?" she teased.

"Yes ma'am, there was lots of stuff left in the store." Little Missy searched through the pile. "I didn't even get a chance to choose, but I absolutely love everything." She held up a cluster of clothing, " I have jeans and shirts and shorts and…and sneakers. Look, Miss Odessa, look!"

"Good heavens above, child, I didn't know new clothes would make you so happy."

"I can finally dress properly for farm work, but it's not just the new clothes, Miss Odessa, Mother and Father are coming." Little Missy turned toward the doorway. "Tell her Grandmother, tell her how you tricked Mr. Tucker."

Mrs. Carter entered the room with a smirk on her face. "I dangled the bait in front of Hershel and he took it, hook, line and sinker." She made no effort to conceal her amusement. "All I had to do was feed his ego and then it was as easy as spreading softened butter."

"Oh, I was right." Miss Odessa drew a deep breath, nodded her head and slowly exhaled. She crossed her arms and said, "I figured you had something to do with Mr. Tucker's sudden change of heart. Miss Beff Anne called and said he had called Mr. Benton and insisted on him taking over his position as soon as possible."

"Did Elizabeth Anne say when they would arrive?"

"Naw, but from the excitement in her voice, I wouldn't be surprised if dey show up for breakfast in the morning."

Little Missy stopped rambling through the clothes and looked up. Grandmother Kate and Miss Odessa were celebrating and she wanted to celebrate this noteworthy occasion too, but she couldn't shake the nagging fear that plagued her. Would this move make her mother happy? The uncertainty hampered her joy.

Chapter 7

Dressed as usual, in a tailored suit and tie, Benton Langford sat at the other end of the supper table, across from his mother-in-law. His first week as the incoming President of the First State Bank proved to be more of a social event rather than work related. He had been introduced to each board member and employee, but had not been given the opportunity to take over the reigns yet. Hershel Tucker still occupied the large office, but he had a desk set up for Benton in the smaller office across from Mrs. Holcomb. This procedure of stepping into his new position was unusual to say the least. Usually there was a farewell speech from the outgoing president and a handshake and then it was business as usual, but not so in this case. Benton was trying to convince himself that this small town atmosphere warranted an adjustment on his part, but he was having a difficult time in knowing how to handle the situation without being viewed as disrespectful or condescending. He had overheard some whispers about him being highfalutin and unable to relate to the plight of the common man. He was finding this unjust perception of him difficult to swallow. He was also finding it difficult to be a long-term guest in his mother-in-law's home. He was used to being the master of the household and was unaccustomed to being confined to one room.

"We couldn't ask for better accommodations," he said, placing his napkin on his lap. He fidgeted with his tie and then proceeded with caution, hoping not to offend his hostess. "It's not that we aren't enjoying our stay and…" he looked directly at Miss Odessa and swept his hand across the table, "and all these delicious meals, but I feel it would be best if we live closer to town, maybe within walking distance to the bank." He turned to his wife and covered her hand with his. "We could definitely get used to all this pampering, couldn't we dear?"

"Most definitely." Elizabeth Anne lifted her eyes and gently pulled her smooth, tiny hand away from his. She looked every bit the image of a sophisticated, perfectly dressed, adoring wife, sitting next to her handsome husband, but her image didn't match the turmoil boiling up from the pit of her stomach. She picked up her fork, flipped it over and chose her words carefully. "I wish we didn't have to move," she half whispered, trying to keep her voice from shaking. She didn't want to sound as if she was contradicting her husband. "But we have all our furniture in storage." She shot her mother a pleading look, begging her to understand. "We won't be moving right away," she spoke slowly. "Maybe you could help me find a house."

"Of course," Mrs. Carter said, making no effort to hide her disappointment. "I'll be happy to help you, but y'all have barely gotten settled and I was hoping…" She noticed the distraught look on her daughter's face so she stopped in mid sentence. "Oh, never mind." She waved her hand in front of her face, trying to erase her hastily spoken words. "I'm just grateful to have y'all here in Shadow Springs…I'll count my blessings and remind myself that my daughter is all grown up with a family of her own." She scooted her chair closer to the table. "We could talk to Hattie Franklin, her husband works in the Probate Office, he'll know about houses that are for sale."

Little Missy hadn't considered the possibility of not living in her grandmother's house. She did not want to move.

With doleful eyes, she stared at her mother and then at her father. "Where will we live?" she asked woefully, bringing a cloud of discomfort to the conversation. Her question hung in the air, waiting for her parents to answer. "Where will we live?" she asked again.

"Well, I'm not sure." Mr. Langford stammered.

"Have you considered the old Richardson Estate?" Mr. Dodie spoke up. "Dat house has been empty for awhile and it's close to town, within spitting distance of the bank."

Elizabeth Anne placed her fork next to her plate and ran her finger around the outer rim. She looked up. "What happened to Yolanda Richardson? Wasn't she accused of killing her husband?

Did she go to jail?"

"Naw, the law didn't bring a case against her. Most of her accusers were naysayers and gossips. I never did put no stock in their tales." Mr. Dodie shook his head. "It all seemed a little far fetched to me."

"Lord have mercy, Dodie." Miss Odessa squeezed her husband's arm. "It's a bewilderment to me why you continue to ignore the facts when dey are staring you in the face." She plopped both elbows on the table and widened her eyes. "The sheriff said Missus Yolander claimed her man jest up and left her and everything he owned. She claimed he went on an extended sea voyage. She said the only thing he took with him was a golden candlestick; sheriff thought dat was what she used to kill him. He said…"

"Odessa, Odessa." Mr. Dodie butted in. "Why are you repeating old gossip? You know the sheriff never found his body. The truth might be he sold dat candlestick and bought hisself a one-way ticket to a place far, far away."

"Or it could be, Dodie Frazier, dat she whacked him over the head with dat candlestick and buried his body under the flo boards of the parlor. Dats the way I heard the story told."

"Well, jest cause dats the way you heard it don't mean dat it's true." Mr. Dodie grinned. "The truth is, Mister Richardson's wife was a strange one. She was mighty strange."

"And how would you know dat?" Miss Odessa shook her finger at her husband. "You only had one encounter with her."

"Dat one encounter was all I needed." He nodded. "Her husband hired me to convert the space under the stairway into a darkroom. He said he was a photographer afore he met his wife and he wanted to take it up again, but his missus wasn't gonna stand for it. She paraded down those stairs, her face painted up worser than Jezebel and wearing an outlandish looking outfit, problee something she had worn during her stage performing days. She commenced to barking out orders and insisting dat her plight in life was to teach the performing arts to an uncultured society." Mr. Dodie shuddered. "She was domineering and bossy and I don't blame her husband one bit. I problee would have runned away from her, too."

"Do you really think he ran away?" Elizabeth Anne asked, slightly amused by the humorous raillery. "Do you think he'll come back someday?"

"Not if he's dead, he won't," Miss Odessa stated. "The house is boarded up. It's empty and void and dats the way I think it should stay."

"Now, Odessa, dat ain't no way to be. Dat house is too nice to set vacant. I don't think it would take too much to fix it up real nice."

Elizabeth Anne drew a deep breath. "I've always been curious about that old mansion." She exhaled slowly. "Grady and I peeked into the windows once."

"What were you and Grady doing there?" Grandmother Kate asked, her voice laden with misgivings.

"We weren't being mischievous." Elizabeth Anne looked at her mother and then she cut her eyes toward Miss Odessa. "Remember Madam Pauline?" she asked. Her voice relaxed. Her demeanor became calm.

"The fortuneteller?" Miss Odessa straightened her neck. "Y'all went to dat palm reader? Miss Beff Anne, I can't believe y'all would do such a thing! Didn't I warn y'all bout the evils of black magic?"

"Calm down, Miss Odessa, we were walking past Madam Pauline's Mystic Parlor, going to Joyce Hester's house because her cousin, Caroline, was visiting from Mississippi."

"Oh, yeah, I remember Joyce and her sneaky cousin." Miss Odessa rubbed the bottom of her chin. "I'll never forget dat puny, little, green-eyed thief." Her face wrinkled. "On one of her visits here I caught her swiping a double handful of my dried apples. Thief, dats what she was, pure and simple."

"Well, I don't remember anything about Caroline being a thief, but I do remember Grady and I sneaking past Madam Pauline's. We were careful not to make any noise or alert her because we didn't want her to come out and cast a spell or place a curse on us. We had almost made it, but suddenly a black cat ran out in front of us. It startled me. Grady tried to muffle my screams but Madam Pauline's gypsy husband must have heard us because he burst out the door with a bullwhip, started zapping this way and that way, knocking over milk bottles and flowerpots. He accused us of being the devil's culprits and threatened to lash us within an inch of our lives and string us up by our toenails. His thunderous intimidation scared us both so badly we aimlessly ran and ran and ran. The first shelter we came to..." Elizabeth pushed her plate forward, "was the old Richardson Estate."

Little Missy's curiosity peaked; she was fascinated by her mother's wild story. She wanted to hear every detail but it bothered her how easily and openly she spoke about Grady Dewberry, her old boyfriend. She seemed to enjoy reminiscing about their past and worse yet, Little Missy's father didn't seem to be bothered by it. He was smiling and listening attentively.

"What happened next?" Little Missy asked, trying not to sound overly curious. She had promised to control her curious streak and she was trying her very best to do so, but her mother's tale had awakened the sleeping giant within her.

"Next, we hid under the high end of the porch and remained there until we were sure we were safe. It seemed like hours but in reality it was probably only a few minutes."

"And then..." Little Missy couldn't stop herself. She had to ask. She couldn't fight the urge any longer. She had to know. "Did the crazy lady come out swinging a golden candlestick?"

"No, silly." Elizabeth Anne laughed light-heartedly and so did everyone at the table. "We decided to peek inside, to see if the old mansion lived up to its reputation. Mr. and Mrs. Richardson bought it from the original builder who had been a very wealthy businessman. He had prided himself on owning an extravagant showpiece." She looked at her husband. "You might want to consider it. It really is a nice home, high ceiling and an impressive staircase."

"Ah," Benton answered, showing no emotion. "It could be a possibility, if it's close enough to the bank and if the renovations aren't too excessive."

"Are you saying we might live there?" Little Missy didn't want to hear that. "But what about the parlor floor? Were the floorboards loose? What if that man is dead or what if he isn't dead and he comes back? What if..."

"I just said it could be a possibility, Katherine," her father answered sternly. "Now, we need to postpone this conversation and carry on with our meal. Our food is getting cold and we aren't being proper guest to our hostess." He looked toward the other end of the table. "Mrs. Carter, please forgive our lack of manners."

Later that night, before going upstairs, Little Missy stopped at her parent's bedroom door. A dim light shown underneath, she hoped they were still awake. She wanted to continue the Richardson Estate conversation. She didn't want to move, she hoped to convince them to stay.

"Katherine, why aren't you in bed?" her father asked, stepping out from the library.

"I was about to knock," she said. "I want to talk…about moving."

"Okay, but don't disturb your mother. Let her rest." He motioned for his daughter to join him in the library. "I know you don't want to move but…"

"Why can't we stay, Father?" Katherine interrupted. "Grandmother's house is huge and there are plenty of rooms and Miss Odessa and Mr. Dodie take such good care of us."

"That's true, honey, but there are some things you may be too young to understand." He sat down on the sofa. "Home is where your family is."

"I know, but if we all stayed here…" Her voice trailed off. She could tell from her father's expression he would let her have her say, but his mind was made up. "Mother seems happier here. Didn't you hear it in her voice tonight when she was telling her story?" Little Missy sat down next to her father and absent-mindedly began to twist the hem of her dress. "Father, I understand more than you think." She stopped twisting and rested her hands in her lap. "I know Mother is mourning the loss of a baby." She lifted her eyes. "I heard her and Grandmother talking and I know you took this job because you thought living here would make her happy again." Tears stung her eyes. She struggled to keep her composure.

"Oh, sweet Katherine." Her father pulled her close to him. "Yes, your mother and I are mourning the loss of a child, a son. She feels she has disappointed me because there can be no more children."

"Why wasn't I told?" She pulled away.

"We thought you...we were trying to spare you the heartache."

"But my heart does ache, from all the secrets, from not knowing."

"I see that now. It was a mistake to keep it from you."

"And don't you see that it would be a mistake to move, to take Mother away from the place that makes her happy? When she's here, in this house, and when she's remembering her childhood, she's happy." Little Missy wiped the corners of her eyes. "I'm afraid if we move her sadness will overtake her and never set her free."

"We can't free her from her sadness, honey. We have to let your mother work that out for herself. Her doctor said it isn't uncommon for a woman who has lost a baby to go through a depression." Her father stood up. "I think finding and decorating a new home would take her mind off of her sorrow. It would give her a purpose...she could rekindle some of her old friendships and..."

Little Missy stiffened. She stopped listening. The mere mention of old friendships set her on alert. She was tempted to ask her father if he knew about Grady Dewberry, if he knew people thought he still carried a torch for his first love. She was tempted to tell him she didn't like it when her mother talked about Grady but she decided not to say anything. She decided to wait; she might be making a mountain out of a molehill.

Chapter 8

Katherine Carter hurried into the foyer with her hat in her hand and her purse dangling from her wrist. She looked through the front windows and called loudly, "Odessa, James Everett is here." She walked to the hall table and picked up her car keys. "I'll let him in on my way out," she yelled, making her way toward the entrance. She opened the screen door and waited for the young boy to walk up the porch steps.

"Good morning, Mrs. Carter," he said cheerfully. "Are you headed somewhere?"

"Yes, sweetie, I'm going to the church."

"Church, on Friday?"

"Yes, the church's banquet room. That's where we're having Mr. Tucker's retirement party."

"Oh, so, he really is gonna retire. Travis and me have been wondering if he had done changed his mind. We seen him going into the bank early every morning last week." James Everett held the door for Mrs. Carter and stepped aside. "We've been hauling lumber for Mr. Emmett's new barn."

"Oh, I had forgotten about Emmett's barn. He has been planning that for a while now, hasn't he?"

"Yes ma'am, bout a year."

"And that's about the same amount of time it's going to take me to get Hershel's retirement party done and over with. He has come up with excuse after excuse, prolonging his leaving." She stopped at the top step and motioned for James Everett to go inside. "Odessa is in the kitchen, she's getting your package ready." She grabbed onto the rail and turned around. "Little Missy has finished her chores for today; why don't you take her with you?"

"But…uh, Mrs. Carter. I don't…"

"Please, do it as a favor to me." Mrs. Carter winked. "She needs to get out and about in the community and…maybe after church on Sunday you could introduce her to some of the other children. Little Missy is used to private schools, she's a little reserved. She doesn't always make a good first impression when approaching new friendships."

James Everett agreed with that statement wholeheartedly, but his mind went into a spin; he desperately wanted to come up with an excuse so he wouldn't have to spend time with the spoiled little rich girl. He didn't want to become her tutor or her mentor. "I," he stammered.

"Oh, thank you, sweetie. You're a godsend, yes you are!" Mrs. Carter waved and rushed down the stairs.

James Everett shook his head as he watched her drive away. "Roped into another catastrophe," he muttered.

The house was quiet except for the muffled sound of dishes rattling in the kitchen. He slowly made his way through the foyer, taking time to admire the coved ceiling, dentil crown molding and the finely crafted curved staircase. Light shining through the high windows in the dining room streaked across the floor in a crisscross pattern. A rainbow of colors reflected off the crystal chandelier and filled the entire room with tiny sparkles. James Everett fought to keep his admiration from becoming envy.

"Hello," he called out. "Mrs. Frazier, it's me, James Everett. Mrs. Carter let me in."

Miss Odessa pushed open the pocket doors and stuck her head out of the kitchen. "Come on back, child, I've got it ready for you."

James Everett took one more quick look around and then forced himself to concentrate on the task at hand. "Mama sent her box last week. She put in some extra butter and a few more eggs. She said the good Lord had sent her an increase so she was gonna pass it on."

"Dat sound jest like your mama." Miss Odessa folded the box lids together and slid the string over the top. "Dat should do the trick till you deliver it but make sure Miss Ella can open it afore you leave." She pointed to a chair. "Have a seat," she said. "Would you like something to eat? Are you hungry?"

"No ma'am, I've already had breakfast, hours ago." He looked around. Little Missy was nowhere in sight. He was glad; maybe he could sneak off without her. "Well, I better hurry on," he said, reaching for the box. "No sense in making poor Miss Ella wait. She says she don't need nothing, but I see her cupboards and…and they are as bare as bare can be." He tucked the box under his arm and headed for the back porch.

Miss Odessa smiled and said, "Be sure and tell Miss Ella I said hello."

James Everett turned. "Yes ma'am, I sure will." He backed out, hoping to make a quick escape, but when he turned around he discovered Little Missy sitting in the swing, her arms folded and a sour look on her face.

"What took you so long?" she asked, slowly standing to her feet. "I've been waiting, Grandmother Kate said I have to go with you."

"I know." James Everett forced the words from between his tightly clenched teeth. He returned her sour look. "She asked me to take you as a favor to her, but if you don't want to go," he sneered, "you can stay here. It ain't no skin off my nose."

"I wasn't given a choice," Little Missy sneered back. "And I don't even know where we're going."

"To Miss Ella's." James Everett shoved the screen door, bolted down the steps and stomped off, not slowing down or turning around to see if she was following him.

"Wait." Little Missy caught the door before it slammed, but hesitated before descending the steps. She considered letting him march off without her, she could defend her defiance by telling her grandmother of his rudeness.

"Come on," he yelled, speeding up. "We ain't got all day."

"I'm coming." She spat the words. Her tolerance of despicable people had never been tested so greatly. He was rude, insensitive, impatient and an over-bearing know-it-all. "Wait, slow down," she demanded, sprinting toward him as fast as she could. He had veered off the path and had disappeared into the woods, barely visible through the overgrowth.

"Where are we going?" she asked, struggling to keep up. She was scared; the trail was dark and the ground was uneven. Her thin knee-length pants and sleeveless blouse offered no protection from the limbs and bushes her guide recklessly turned loose of as he pushed through in front of her.

"Hey, watch it," she pleaded. "I don't know the way. Please, can't you slow down?"

"Can't you do anything besides whine?" He stopped and turned around. "You're turning a pleasant job into a chore. I like visiting with Miss Ella." He lifted the box. "She needs this."

Little Missy stumbled but regained her balance. "Who is this lady and why in the world does she choose to live in the middle of this uninhabitable forest and all these irritating vines and bushes?"

"Miss Ella is…well…Mama says Miss Ella is the definition of misfortune. She was orphaned at thirteen, when pneumonia killed both her parents within three days of each other. Her only living relative, an aunt from someplace up north, was gonna move down here and finish raising her but when she found out about Miss Ella's disability she abandoned that idea and turned her over to the state." James Everett's voice softened. "When she got too old for the state home, they turned her out, left her to fend for herself. She would have starved had it not been for Miss Mary Louise Perkins. Miss Mary Louise was mission minded. She never married or had children of her own, but she had compassion for wayward souls. I guess she figured Miss Ella was as wayward as a soul could get, so she took her in. She became her benefactor until she died…and after that…Miss Ella became a ward of the community." James Everett motioned toward the box. "Most every family takes turns fixing her a package."

"What's in the package?"

"Food, mostly, but sometimes, especially around Christmas, warm clothes and socks are added."

"I do hope guns, bullets, and a snake killing weapon has been included, too, because it is apparent that anyone who lives in this wilderness will need all three."

James Everett laughed, not a forced laugh, but an honest to goodness laugh. "None of those things would be of any value to Miss

Ella."

Little Missy was caught off-guard. She didn't see the humor in her statement. "Why do you say that? Why are you laughing?"

"You'll see," he said, trying to keep a straight face. "You'll see."

The words, smart aleck, hung on the tip of Little Missy's tongue. She forced herself to remain quiet even though she was tempted to give James Everett Holloway a piece of her mind. Common sense convinced her that tolerance would be far more beneficial; lessening the time she had to spend with him. Bickering back and forth could go on for hours, but the decision to keep her mouth shut was a hard pill to swallow. She fought the urge to tell him off until they came to the railroad tracks.

"We'll walk the tracks the rest of the way." James Everett jumped off the small embankment. He set the box down and extended his hand. "Here, let me help you. Don't want you to turn an ankle or break a leg. I can't tote you and the box, too."

"Never mind," Little Missy said, sarcastically pushing his hand away. "I don't need your help." She sat down and scooted her body to the edge of the bank and then pushed off, sliding to the bottom. "See, I didn't need your assistance." She made a face and dusted her backside.

"Makes no difference to me how you get down the bank, but you're gonna have to keep up." James Everett looked up and down the tracks. "There ain't much room to get off in case a train comes barreling down on us and you're gonna have to walk mighty fast once we get to the trestle…it's a fifty foot drop to the water below." He picked up the box, stepped over the rail and briskly took long strides up the center of the tracks. "Come on," he yelled over his shoulders. "A train might be headed this way!"

"A train, fifty foot drop…hey, wait!" Little Missy rushed to catch up. "Did Grandmother Kate know you would be bringing me this way or are you just doing this to scare me?" She breathed heavily. "I'm certain she wouldn't knowingly put my life at risk."

"Oh, for Pete's sake, it's just a little ways and besides it's much shorter this way. I didn't figure you would want to walk three miles." He turned. "You got a problem with taking the shortcut?"

"Well no, I don't, but I do have a problem with your attitude. I see no sense in alarming me unnecessarily."

James Everett shook his head. "Ain't trying to alarm you, just making sure you can run if we need to." He turned forward and pointed. "See that up ahead? That's the trestle."

A huge skeleton of iron beams, rails and crossties loomed ahead. The rusty structure stretched several hundred feet across a creek surrounded by high banks. There were no guardrails or detour points between one end and the other, just a deep pool of water, high concrete pylons protruding from the creek floor and a crisscross of wooden supports extending up and under the old relic.

"This thing doesn't look safe," Little Missy whispered, cautiously stomping her foot to test its sturdiness. "When was it built?"

"Don't know," James Everett answered, without hesitation or slowing down. "It's old, that's for sure."

"Do trains really travel over this? Isn't anyone concerned about safety?"

"Yeah, there has been talk about replacing it, but that's all, just talk," he shouted backward.

"Well, I'm afraid. I'm not sure I want to…"

"Suit yourself, ain't no skin off my nose." James Everett kept walking. "I sure hope you can find your way back and be sure and tell your grandmother…"

"Oh, hush up," Little Missy interrupted. "I'm coming." She ran, careful not to make a misstep. Once she caught up with James Everett, she wedged closely between him and the outer rail. The view over the edge was frightening. "How deep is the water?"

"Uh…maybe eight to ten feet. It's deep enough to dive from the creek bank. Me and Travis have done it a million times."

"Why would you do that?" Little Missy's legs were weary. She stuck out her arm, forcing her companion to come to a halt.

"Because it's our swimming hole." He was irritated. "Everybody swims there." He looked sideways and pushed her arm down. "Come Labor Day it'll be more crowded than a can of sardines."

"Why?" she asked, gasping to catch her breath.

"I don't know. Why are you asking such crazy questions?" He

held his hand up to his ear and listened for a train. "Are you stalling for time?" James Everett nervously looked up and down the tracks. "We need to go, like I already told you…"

"I know," Little Missy nodded. "I'm ready now."

They quickly made their way to the end of the trestle and around the bend before going down a bank and onto an old dirt road.

"This way leads back to the highway and this way," James Everett took a left, "leads to Miss Ella's." He placed his finger to his lips. "We have to be quiet, don't want to spook her. We don't want her coming after us with all those guns, bullets and snake killing weapons."

"Are you being pretentious?" Little Missy set her eyes. "You are so pious and condescending, I never know when you're telling the truth."

Staring back, eye to eye, James Everett puffed his chest. "I always tell the truth…according to me." He smiled. "And the truth is that your big words and fancy talk don't impress me none. You ain't never done nothing, you don't know how to do nothing. You're clueless."

"And you are…you're mean, you're despicable, you're aggravating…and you're rude…look at you…walking away when I'm talking to you." She shook her fist.

"You coming?" he called over his shoulder.

The yard was broom-swept, neat and clean, but it was divided into sections by long ropes. All the ropes were attached, one just above the other, to the wall next to the front door. They led the way to the porch railing but then each separated in a different direction. One led to the old shed, another to the outhouse and another to the well and woodpile. A wire fence formed a boundary, not to keep out intruders but to distinguish the yard from the forest. There was no mailbox, no power line and no flowerbeds.

The house, little more than a shack, was constructed of rough-cut sawmill lumber. Poles made from small trees that had the limbs cut off and the bark removed supported the porch. The chimney was made of rocks, matching the pillar foundation and one lone oak tree stood at the edge of the yard. A large dinner bell hung from its lowest branch.

James Everett immediately ran to the oak tree and began to ring the bell. "Miss Ella, Miss Ella," he called. "It's me, I have your package."

Little Missy stood at the edge of the road. She was spellbound; she had never seen anything like this. She wasn't sure what to make of it.

"Why the ropes?" she whispered loudly.

James Everett did not answer; instead he shot her an angry look and motioned her forward. She slowly crept behind him and latched onto the back of his shirt, determined not to turn loose.

The front door slowly opened and a very thin, wiry haired, fragile old lady, resembling the classic description of a fairytale witch stepped outside. "My friend," she called, grasping the top rope and then sliding her feet, feeling her way to the edge of the porch. She stopped when her foot reached the step off. "Come, come," she beckoned, obviously excited about having a visitor. "It gets mighty lonely here," she said.

"Yes, ma'am." James Everett moved forward, tugging at his shirt, struggling to free himself from Little Missy's death grip. "Let go," he ordered in a low whisper.

"No." Little Missy rebelled, digging her feet into the dirt. "No, what's wrong with her? I'm scared."

"Oh, you're such a…she's blind. She ain't gonna hurt you." James Everett held up the box. "I brought your package, Miss Ella."

"Oh, bless your heart." The old lady reached out, feeling the air. "The Lord has blessed me more than I can count…good friends and generous neighbors." She motioned him forward. "I recognize your voice, James Everett, but I don't know your companion. Who do you have with you?"

Little Missy's eyes widened. "How did she know?" she whispered softly.

"She's blind, but she ain't deaf," James Everett whispered back, and then he jerked free. "Her name is," he spoke loudly, "uh, I forgot what her real name is, but she wants to be called Little Missy."

"Well then, come here, Little Missy, and let me see what you look like." Miss Ella stretched her wrinkled hands and wiggled her long bony fingers. "Let me feel your face, child." She smiled, turning her head from side to side, listening for footsteps. "Come here."

The storybook, Hansel and Gretel, flashed into Little Missy's mind, causing her to panic. She silently mouthed the word no, rapidly shook her head and stepped back. She desperately wanted to escape, but James Everett grabbed her with his free hand and dragged her up the steps. He sat the box down and pushed her forward, maneuvering her face into the old lady's hands.

Little Missy fought to remain calm. She closed her eyes, so she wouldn't have to look at the lady's smoke-rimmed, cloudy eyes and wrinkled, leathery skin. She tried to ignore the cold fingers tracing her face, the rough calluses sliding across her cheeks and the unpleasant smell of body odor. Her rapid heartbeat and labored breathing made her feel faint. She drew her shoulders inward, stiffened her knees, and prayed they would support her if she were to succumb to the dizziness that threatened to cause her to pass out. She was nervous, her lungs ached and she felt lightheaded. "I…I," she gasped. "I need to sit down."

"Of course you do," Miss Ella agreed. "I was about to suggest that very thing. Your face is clammy and you're sweating." She called out, "James Everett, please help this poor girl. It is obvious, even to a blind woman, that she is very delicate and isn't used to hot weather."

Little Missy crumpled to the floor. "Yes, ma'am, it's the weather." She mumbled, struggling to think of a logical excuse. "And…and… James Everett made me walk very fast over the train trestle." She blew out her breath and quickly breathed in again. "I'm just not accustomed to such strenuous activity."

"Oh my, do you need a drink of water?"

"Yes, please, that would be lovely."

Miss Ella followed the rope back to the porch wall and felt for the shelf that held the water bucket.

"Here, let me do that," James Everett rushed over and got a dipper full of water and carried it to Little Missy. He shoved it toward her and squinted his eyes. "You poor little delicate flower," he mocked. "You're about to melt in this nasty heat." He made a face and then led Miss Ella inside, leaving Little Missy to compose herself.

She was relieved to have a moment to gather her thoughts. She needed time to think about the way she had acted toward Miss Ella. It was not her nature to be disrespectful, but she had been taken by surprise. She had not been forewarned.

She lingered, slowly sipping the water and letting it drizzle down the back of her throat. She was grateful for the cool refreshment, so freely offered by someone who had so little. Little Missy truly was sorry. If only she had known what to expect. James Everett should have prepared her. He was just as much to blame for her actions as she was and she intended to tell him that the first chance she got.

She pondered the situation briefly, but decided her new acquaintance might perceive her as being standoffish if she stayed on the porch too long, so she picked up the box and quickly made her way to the front door. It was ajar so she stepped inside without knocking. James Everett was sitting at the table, facing Miss Ella; his back was toward the door.

"Have you been able to remember anything new? It's very important." He leaned closer. "I know Daddy didn't kill himself. Somebody killed him, but I ain't figured out who or why. Do you remember his exact words?"

"Not his exact words, but your daddy told me he had discovered some wrongdoing. He said he was going to do some more snooping before he told Sheriff Connelly." Miss Ella stopped. She listened. "Someone has joined us. Is that you, Little Missy?"

James Everett jerked around. "This is a private conversation."

"I'm sorry," Little Missy lowered her eyes. "I didn't mean to interrupt but you forgot the box. I thought maybe I should bring it in."

"No, go away." James Everett's voice was filled with anger. "This is none of your business. "Go." He pointed outside.

"I'm sorry." Little Missy cringed at his sharpness. "I…I…"

Miss Ella reached across the table and grabbed James Everett's arm. She squeezed tightly and shook her head. "This ain't like you. You have never acted this way before. That young lady ain't your enemy, James Everett." She released his arm and stood up. "What would your mama think if she knew you were acting this way? What about Travis? You know your preacher brother wouldn't like your behavior one bit. Now, would he?"

"No ma'am, he wouldn't," James Everett answered, showing respect for Miss Ella. "But he ain't a preacher yet."

"I know Travis ain't been to Bible college yet but that don't matter. He comes by and lets me hear his practice sermons and I can tell you this for a fact, he's a fine preacher already and he would not approve of the way you are acting." She felt for her chair and eased back down. "I think you should consider apologizing."

"Yes, ma'am, I will."

"You will what? You'll apologize to Little Missy?"

James Everett cleared his throat. "I'll consider it."

Miss Ella's voice relaxed. "You can't bear this burden alone and you need more help than this old blind woman can give you." She stared in the direction of the door and waved her hand, motioning Little Missy forward. "Would you be willing to help?" she asked.

Little Missy walked to the table. "Yes, ma'am, I will. I've been curious about Mr. Holloway's death too. Miss Odessa and I have discussed it and she doesn't believe he killed himself either."

"See, James Everett," Miss Ella replied. "It looks like you have a willing partner. What do you say, can she join us?"

"I don't know. She's headstrong and she ain't much good at nothing. She don't know how to…"

"But I can learn," Little Missy interrupted. "I learned to do my chores, didn't I?" She put the box down and pulled out a chair.

"Yeah, but…"

"Please, I promise to do what you tell me." She sat down and scooted closer to the table. "I've been curious about what happened to your daddy. I really want to know."

"Me too," James Everett confided. "I guess you can help…what did Miss Odessa say?"

"She said it didn't make sense to her why your daddy would kill himself after he'd work so hard to stop drinking, after he got a job and was finally being the man he …" Little Missy quickly covered her mouth with her hand. "I'm sorry, I didn't mean any disrespect."

"That's okay, I know what folks thought of my daddy. They thought he was a sorry drunk." He lowered his eyes. "I ain't gonna make excuses for him." James Everett looked up. "I was ashamed of him most of the time, but he was my daddy…drunk or sober, he was still my daddy. I had to respect him even when he didn't deserve it." He bit his lip. "Many of the things folks said about him were true, but I just can't accept the idea of him killing himself. I know he wouldn't do that."

Little Missy refused to let her face show emotion, she did not want to show feelings of sorrow. She knew James Everett was prideful; he would not welcome her feeling sorry for him. "Miss Odessa said you found him…behind Mr. Tucker's barn."

James Everett nodded in acknowledgement. "Daddy worked for Mr. Tucker, so I don't have a problem with him being behind the barn but, why? Of all the places, why would he go there? And why would he use Mr. Tucker's gun? Daddy owned a handgun and a shotgun."

"Did anybody ask Mr. Tucker about it?"

"Yeah, Sheriff Connelly did and so did Travis. He told them Daddy had asked him if he could use it for target practice, but that don't make sense either. Daddy was a sure shot. I've hunted with him many times and he didn't miss. He said bullets where too expensive to waste." James Everett whispered, "He also told them that he had noticed Daddy acting depressed and downhearted. He said he had no idea Daddy was planning to do something like that. He said he wished he'd never loaned him his gun, he wished he'd kept it locked up in his office desk."

"Did you notice your father acting differently?"

"Yeah, but not depressed. He acted kinda like his mind was far away, on something else."

"Yes." Miss Ella joined the conversation. "That's the way I'd describe him, too. He brought me a load of stove wood, quickly unloaded it and rushed off, barely giving me the time of day. He said he didn't have time to explain, but he'd found what he had been looking for and he had hidden it. He didn't tell me what it was or where he hid it, but he said, 'It's under your nose,'" and then he gave me that handkerchief."

"What handkerchief?" Little Missy shot James Everett a confused look.

"This one." He pulled it from his back pocket and placed it on the table. "It's a woman's lace handkerchief." He said, gently unwrapping it from the plastic wrapping. "Here." He poked it under Little Missy's nose. "Smell it. It smells good."

She took a big whiff. "That is A Joyful Rose, my mother wears that perfume. It's expensive. Do you know who the handkerchief belongs to?"

"Nope."

"I wonder...." Little Missy's brow furrowed. "How does the handkerchief play into this puzzlement?"

"I've wondered that too," James Everett admitted.

Chapter 9

The children left Miss Ella's home with a sense of urgency. There were many missing pieces of the puzzle, many unanswered questions. The mystery could not be solved without much study, so they agreed to concentrate on finding out as much as possible as soon as possible. James Everett was so deep in thought he didn't notice they had passed the shortcut until Little Missy stopped him. She pointed down the dirt road. "This way leads to town, right?"

"Yeah," James Everett answered. "Why?"

"Because I want to go to the old Richardson Estate, do you know where it is?"

"Sure, it's the mansion on the hill, overlooking the town. Why do you want to go there?"

"I actually want to go inside." Little Missy straightened her shoulders. "Since I may be living there, I want to see what the inside looks like."

"You want to go inside?" James Everett bellowed with annoyance. "Are you crazy? Do you know the story about that old house?"

"I know about Yolanda Richardson, if that's what you're talking about." Little Missy slung her head to the side and pretended she wasn't uneasy about what Miss Odessa had said about Mr. Richardson being buried under the parlor floor. "I know about her husband and the golden candlestick and…and all that other stuff." She waved her hands, dismissing his remarks as frivolous.

"Well, do you know you can't just waltz in there because you want to? That place is boarded up tighter that a jail cell on Saturday night."

"What do you mean?"

"I mean, that place was broke into so many times by folks looking for the candlestick and other treasures that the sheriff had it boarded up. He stuck signs up everywhere, warning jail time if anybody's caught trespassing." James Everett pulled at Little Missy's arm. "We need to go back."

"We…don't need to do anything." She swatted his hand away. "You can go back if you want to, but I intend to go to the old mansion. I'm not afraid of going to jail."

"Oh, I guess you think your daddy will pull some strings for you." James Everett's face reddened. "The law don't mean nothing to the rich."

"No, I don't think that." She blinked. Tears filled her eyes. "Why do you have to be so mean?" She choked back her resentment and pressed her quivering lips together. "From the first day we met you have been nasty and hateful toward me. Why do you dislike me?"

James Everett gasped. Her words hit hard, like a slap in the face. It was difficult to admit, but her depiction of him was accurate. He had been mean and unkind. Even Miss Ella, through her world of darkness, saw his cruelty and she had called his hand on it.

"I'm sorry." His throat tightened. "I don't dislike you. I…I…" James Everett ran his hand through his hair, unaware that he did that every time he felt uncomfortable.

"Well, you sure act like you do." Little Missy dabbed the corners of her eyes. "You told Miss Ella that I was good at nothing. You said I…"

"I know what I said," James Everett interjected loudly, but quickly lowered his voice. "I spoke out of turn." He focused his attention on his bare feet. "You seem to have everything, you don't know what it's like to hurt, to be ashamed of who you are." He lifted his eyes. "You have no idea what it's like to have problems."

Little Missy met his gaze. "You're wrong James Everett, I have problems." She sniffed. "Mine aren't the same as yours, but I have problems too."

"Really, what kind?"

"My mother isn't well, my father's job is uncertain and I…I don't have anybody to talk to." She stepped closer. "I pray, but I'm not sure God is listening." This admission was unexpected. Little Missy didn't mean to say the words out loud; she had been wrestling with her feelings for a long time. She needed to feel God's presence; she needed answers that only He could provide. "Sometimes I feel lost, as if I'm wandering in the wilderness like Moses." A tiny stream of tears trickled down her face.

James Everett didn't mean to make her cry. He realized he had mistreated her; he had taken his anger out on her. It wasn't her fault that his family was suffering. She had nothing to do with his tragedy, he could see that now and he was sorry. "I sometimes feel that way too," he admitted, stumbling over his words. "Especially when I think about the bank taking our farm."

Little Missy wiped her tears. "The bank is going to foreclose on your farm?" She blinked, trying to make sure she had understood him. "Why?"

"Mr. Tucker said Daddy missed a lot of payments back when he was drinking…but he was catching up. He said that's why he let Daddy work for him, but now that he's dead…the bank will have no choice but to…to." James Everett scrunched his face and pounded his fist into his hand. "But me and Travis ain't gonna let them. We promised Mama we'd pay every last cent and we aim to keep our promise. We work hard six days a week, ten to twelve hours a day. We're gonna make sure the bank gets its money."

"I didn't know, James Everett. I'm sorry, really I am."

"Don't want no sympathy." He kept his tone even; he wanted to hide the fact that he was embarrassed. He breathed in quickly and forced a smile. "But if you want to go to the old Richardson place, I guess I can take you. I know how to slip through the back gate."

"You'll take me?" Little Missy perked up.

"Yeah, but I'm warning you right now, if we get caught you're on your own. I don't plan on going to jail."

"Me either." She returned his smile. "Me either."

The dirt road was cool and shaded, but the highway was hot and oozing with tar. James Everett walked on the pavement. His feet were tough. Hot tar didn't bother him, but Little Missy walked on the grass. She wanted to safeguard her new sneakers, but his stride, long and fast, left her at a disadvantage. She struggled to keep up, but knew better than to ask him to slow down or to mention that tar would be impossible to remove from her newly purchased shoes.

"Turn this way," James Everett called. He ducked behind some bushes and waited for her to join him. "We have to be quiet, remember we're trying to avoid getting caught."

"I know," Little Missy whispered. Her heart rate increased, she was excited, anxious and a little scared. "How do you know about the back gate?"

"Scuppernongs," James Everett replied.

"Scupper…what?"

"Scuppernongs, they are delicious. Mama makes jelly out of them."

"Okay, but what do scupper…nongs have to do with the…?"

"There is a scuppernong arbor in the backyard. I snuck in one time and gathered a bucket full." He shot her a pleading look. "I would appreciate it if you would keep that fact to yourself. Mama would be disappointed if she knew exactly where I got them."

"Don't worry, I won't tell. I only see her at church anyway, and she's always busy with the twins." Little Missy giggled nervously. "How much further?"

"Just up ahead."

James Everett parted the foliage and led the way through the faded path. He held back the limbs this time, not turning them loose until both had passed through. When they arrived at the iron gate he motioned for Little Missy to stay put while he searched for the place where he had entered before. He followed the gate, feeling the ground with his feet, until he located the shallow trench. "This way," he whispered.

Little Missy rushed over and helped him pull the leaves and debris away until the hole was deep enough for James Everett to crawl underneath. He then ordered her to scoot under on her back and raise her arms so he could pull her through. She did as she was told and within minutes she was on the other side. She looked up and was astounded at what she saw. The yard was wide and expanding, including a rock terrace, a small fruit orchard, the scuppernong arbor and several mature pecan trees. The grounds were much neglected, but the remnants of elaborate flowerbeds, raised rose gardens and sculpted shrubbery revealed evidence of a landscape that had been designed by a master of horticulture.

The mansion rose up two stories from its stone foundation. Wide steps led to an enormous back veranda with huge columns and ornamental wrought iron railings with the same design as the gate. Sets of evenly spaced windows extended across the top and bottom floors and two large coach lantern sconces set on either side of the oversized stained-glass back door.

"This place once was beautiful." Little Missy put her hands up to her face. "Mother is going to love it." Her distress caused James Everett to turn around.

"Is that a bad thing?"

"I don't want to move. I want to stay at my grandmother's house."

"Who says you have to move?"

"My father, he wants to give Mother a house of her own." Little Missy waved her arms. "But this is much more than a house. It's grand."

"Yep, it's grand all right. Ain't no way around that."

Little Missy nodded, her shoulders slumped. "Can we peek inside? Do you think we can climb through a window?"

"We won't know till we try." James Everett hunkered down and darted across the yard. He tried several of the lower windows but they had been nailed shut. He shrugged his shoulders and silently mouthed the words. "Meet me around the front."

The hot, thick air was stifling. Little Missy was sweating, her clothes clung to her skin and her hair lay limp around her neck. The shade of the massive oak trees in the front yard offered no relief so she sought comfort under the high porch. While she waited for James Everett to check the other windows she recalled her mother's story. This had to be the same place where she and Grady had taken refuge from Madam Pauline's husband. Little Missy was amazed by the fact that she was now hiding in the same place, trying not to get caught, and that she too was about to try to peek inside the mansion. This thought-provoking revelation was intriguing. She wanted to mention it to James Everett, but the minute she saw the bleak look on his face she knew something was wrong. "What?" she asked.

"I heard voices." He ran his hand through his hair. "Somebody is in there."

"Who?"

"I don't know." His voice wavered. "I saw a shadowy figure through the window. We've gotta get out of here."

Little Missy's mind flew into frenzy. Not only was she experiencing a deja vu moment from her mother's past, but now she was being drawn into Miss Odessa's version of what happened to Mr. Richardson. "The figure, was it a ghost?"

"Ghost," James Everett repeated.

"Yes, Mr. Richardson's ghost."

"What are you talking about?" He was becoming aggravated. "The figure was of a woman."

"A woman." Little Missy's heart beat hard and fast, pounding in her ears and causing the blood to rush to her brain. "Was it Yolanda Richardson?"

"I don't know who it was…ghost or human, I really don't care." James Everett poked his head out and listened. He hoped to make a run for it but suddenly he heard the front door open, footsteps above them and muffled voices. "We're trapped." He stepped back and grabbed Little Missy by her shoulders. "Be quiet," he warned. She was wide-eyed and pale. James Everett was afraid she was going to faint. "Are you okay?" he whispered.

She nodded and leaned forward, bracing against him. "What are we going to do?"

"We're gonna lay low and listen." James Everett fought to stay calm, fought to control his breathing. The voices were becoming louder and more distinguishable, a male voice and a female voice, but he couldn't make out what was being said.

"Ah," Little Missy made a choking sound.

He cut his eyes toward her and quickly covered her mouth. "Shhh," he scolded.

She squirmed, rolled her eyes and jabbed his side repeatedly until he removed his hand. "That's Mother," she muttered.

"Your mother?"

"Yes, come on."

"No, wait. We're not supposed to be here, remember?"

"Oh, that's okay, I know what to do." Little Missy pulled away and quickly dusted off her clothes. "Mother, Mother, is that you?" she called loudly as she exited the hideout. She flipped the damp strands of hair away from her face and turned. "Come on," she whispered through gritted teeth.

James Everett stared blankly.

"Come on," she said again, her eyebrows raised and her face twisted.

"Katherine, is that you?" Her mother called in a voice full of uncertainty.

"Yes ma'am." The young girl smiled sweetly and marched up the steps. She waited for James Everett. "I was curious to see the house so I asked my friend to bring me here." Little Missy stood next to her mother. "We've already seen the backyard."

"Katherine, I'm surprised to see you." Her mother frowned. "Does your grandmother know where you are?" she questioned, pulling a leaf from her daughter's hair.

Little Missy quickly stepped back, fluffed her hair and brushed bits of trash off her shoulders. "She knows I'm with James Everett." She pushed him forward. "Mother, you remember, we met him on our first visit."

Elizabeth Anne nodded. "Of course, I remember. James Everett, how are you?"

"Fine, ma'am," he answered shyly. "We were…" He shot Little Missy a confused look. "We, ah…"

"We were hoping to see the inside of the house." She stepped forward. "Have you seen it yet?"

"Yes, dear, Mr. Franklin was kind enough to show it to me." She threw up her hands. "Oh, my goodness, where are my manners? Carl, this is my daughter and her friend."

"Nice to meet you," Carl Franklin said, barely glancing in their direction. He looked anxious to get out of the heat. He removed his jacket and loosened his tie. "Mrs. Langford, what do you think?" He mopped his forehead with his shirtsleeve, exposing a large sweat stain under his arm. "Do you like the place?"

"Well, I'm not sure. There are a lot of repairs that need to be made and of course, I'll want my husband to take a look."

"Sure, sure, I can arrange that." He searched his jacket pocket for his handkerchief. "Here, let's have a seat on the steps," he said, pointing with his briefcase. "I brought the information about Mrs. Richardson's next of kin with me. No sense in us walking back down the hill to the car." He used his handkerchief to clean a space for them to sit. "I believe her nephew was the one who probated the will."

Little Missy nudged James Everett and cut her eyes toward the front door. "Follow me," she whispered, using the distraction to slip inside.

"Wow!" James Everett marveled.

"Oh, my." Were the only words that came from Little Missy's lips. She had expected the mansion to be finely crafted but this surpassed her expectations. The foyer led into a grand circular receiving room with rich paneled walls, intricately carved crown molding, high ceilings and tall doorways. An elegant marble fireplace and mantel anchored the wall across from the magnificent winding staircase that wound from the top floor to the bottom floor in a semi-circle of imported mahogany. A wooden ball set atop the large banister post and a shimmering multi-tiered crystal chandelier cascaded down from the medallion above.

She stood, suspended, motionless for what seemed an eternity. She felt defeated. This house was exactly what her father would want. It was grander than any house they had ever lived in, but she was confident it would fit his taste perfectly.

"What are you waiting for?" James Everett asked, staring at her. "We're inside now, where to?"

"Oh, uh, the parlor." She shook her head, trying to clear her mind. "I want to check the parlor floor."

"What for?"

"For evidence of foul play, to see if Mr. Richardson's body…oh, never mind." Little Missy led the way from room to room. They found the servants' quarters, bathrooms, a huge kitchen, dining room and a library on the main floor but no parlor. "Where's the parlor?"

she asked, stopping at the staircase. "Surely it's not upstairs." She looked at James Everett. "How can there be a dead body under the parlor floor if there isn't a parlor?"

"Maybe the crazy lady's husband really did run away or," he answered looking around, "maybe this big room is considered the parlor." James Everett scanned to floor. "Looks solid to me."

"What about next to the fireplace?" Little Missy jerked around. "What about..." her words faded.

James Everett looked up. "What about...oh..." He became mute. An embarrassed grin slowly crept across his face. He cut his eyes toward Little Missy. She was stone faced.

Her mother stood in the doorway. "What are you looking for?" she asked solemnly.

"Uh, the parlor," her daughter answered weakly.

Elizabeth Anne raised her eyebrows and stared ominously. "You want to look for Mr. Richardson's dead body under the parlor floor?" she asked, slowly turning to make sure Mr. Franklin was still waiting on the steps. Then she put her hand to the side of her mouth and whispered. "I've already checked, no parlor and no dead body." She smiled. "Katherine, I swear, your curiosity will be the death of me."

Chapter 10

The evening air was hot and sticky, a sure recipe for limp hair and wilting makeup. Every southern belle had been taught, from a very young age, to avoid being caught in such an uncomplimentary predicament, so the ladies hurried across the church parking lot. Their rush to get inside the banquet room could have been compared to a stampede had it not been for their genteel upbringing. The importance of being prim and proper dictated patience therefore, easing the tense moments as they prepared to make their grand entrance.

Mrs. Katherine Carter stood at the head of the receiving line, welcoming the guest to Hershel Tucker's long-awaited retirement party. She looked lovely in her emerald green dress and sparkling earrings. Her attire enhanced her natural beauty, giving her maturity a youthful glow.

Hershel Tucker sat at the center of the long banquet table, surrounded on both sides by the board of directors and their wives. Little Missy's father, Judge Wilkes and Mayor Digby were politely conversing, seemingly unaware that Charlotte Wilkes and the mayor's wife were distraught over the faux pas they felt their hostess had committed. Their critical assessment lacked merit, but had not prevented them from openly showing their displeasure of what they considered to be a seating blunder. Florence Digby had promptly informed Kate that she felt her husband and the Judge should have been seated closer to the podium. Mrs. Carter, however, had disagreed and had reminded her that Hershel Tucker was the honoree and that she, her husband and the judge and his wife were only invited guest. Kate had then smiled, quickly dismissed her with a wave of her hand and told her to relax and go back and enjoy the party. But Mrs. Digby had been insulted beyond measure. She was outraged that someone like Katherine Carter had the gall to make such a statement so she vowed she would never attend another function hosted by such a rude and insensitive person, to which Kate had replied, "I'm sorry you feel that way but I will happily remove your name from my invitation list."

Little Missy listened to part of the conversation but quickly became bored. She didn't have a seating preference and could not understand why Mrs. Digby was so fired up about who sat where. She would have just as happily stayed home with Miss Odessa and Mr. Dodie had it not been for her fear that the charlatan, Grady Dewberry, would show up and act like a love sick, jilted martyr suffering a life of unhappiness and despair. Little Missy was determined to squash his performance. She was not going to allow him to entice her mother or distract from Mr. Tucker's bon voyage party so she positioned herself in the far corner, next to the side entrance. This lookout point would allow her to watch both, the entrance and her mother, who had dutifully assumed the role of guiding the guest to their assigned tables.

Little Missy had anticipated this evening ever since she'd witness Grandmother Kate coerce Mr. Tucker into allowing her to orchestrate this event. She hoped after tonight he would pack his bags, jump on the first train to Texas and never be heard from again. She hoped her father would become so preoccupied with his new job he would forget all about moving and she hoped her mother would evolve back into the person she used to be. Little Missy was ready to put all her anxieties aside and concentrate on helping James Everett solve the mystery of who killed his daddy. She was also ready to stop worrying about her mother but her behavior earlier that afternoon had been unsettling. She had changed her dress three times and had fussed with her hair for what seemed like hours. She had insisted her appearance had to be perfect; she had to present herself in a way that would be an asset to her husband, the new bank president, but Little Missy was skeptical. She had seen Grady's name on her grandmother's invitation list. She knew he would be at the party and she wondered if maybe her mother's beauty regiment was for his benefit instead…if so, she intended to intervene, to buffer their reunion. Her mother was not herself, Little Missy had to protect her but she didn't know what Mr. Dewberry looked like.

"It might help if I had taken the time to get a description of him," she spoke the words out loud. The room was filling up. The crowd was getting thicker. Many of the guests had left their tables and were standing in the aisles, mingling with the latecomers. They bunched up in clusters. "And it would help if folks would go sit down. I can't see...I can't tell..." She tiptoed and glanced at the clock hanging over the doorway. "Almost time, he's got to be here by now," she huffed. "This isn't going to work."

"What's not going to work, young lady?" a male voice asked.

Little Missy whirled around and shaded her eyes. The setting sun, flooding through the slightly opened door, blinded her. "Excuse me." She squinted. "Are you speaking to me?"

"Well, yes, I thought you were speaking to me."

"No sir, I was talking to myself... I mean, I was thinking out loud." Her voice wavered. She was embarrassed. She wondered how much of her conversation he had overheard.

"I'm glad I'm not the only one who talks to their self." He mused. "I was afraid it was a trait of old age or worse yet, insanity. But since you are obviously not old and don't appear to be insane ...well, I figure we are just kindred spirits, don't you?"

"I guess so," Little Missy answered, relieved by the friendly sound of the stranger's voice. "I usually don't talk to myself but I'm looking for someone."

"Oh, is that so?" The stranger asked, closing the door. He stepped into the light. "Who are you looking for? Maybe I can help, I know almost everybody in town. What does he or she look like?"

"It's a he...but I don't know what he looks like. I forgot to ask." She admitted.

The gentleman standing in front of her was handsome in a way that was difficult to describe. He had dark hair, a ruddy complexion and piercing blue eyes. He was tall and lean, not muscular or intimidating. His smile was endearing, but the rest of his features were common and ordinary. His face was not chiseled nor did he have prominent cheekbones. His demeanor was calming, low-key and nonjudgmental. Little Missy was nervous, not because he made her nervous, but because she realized she was at a loss for words. How could he help her if she couldn't describe who she was looking for?

"Well, let's try this strategy." The stranger grinned. "Since you don't know what he looks like…can you tell me his name?"

"I'd rather not say." Little Missy calmed herself. "I don't want him to know that I'm inquiring about him. I've heard rumors and I'd like to check him out first before meeting him face to face."

"Oh, okay…then I'll point to someone," he stretched his neck and looked around the room, "and you tell me if you want to know his name. Okay?"

"Okay." Little Missy nodded.

"What about the slightly overweight gentleman standing next to the punch bowl or the guy with the gray beard?"

Little Missy shook her head. "They are too old. I'm looking for someone younger."

"Younger, let's see…what about the young man carrying the tray?"

"No, that's Travis Holloway. I know him and his brother. Travis isn't the one, he's too young."

"Okay, first too old and now too young. Let's see…what about…?"

Little Missy followed the stranger's hand, slowly moving across the room. She swept her gaze from person to person, dismissing each one until…until she noticed her mother. She was gracefully sauntering toward them. Her hands were extended and she was smiling sweetly.

"Grady," she said, approaching closer and closer. "So nice of you to come."

Little Missy stood ramrod straight, unable to move, unable to speak. She blinked her eyes. Who was her mother talking to? Surely she wasn't addressing the stranger standing next to her. Surely the stranger wasn't Grady Dewberry…oh, how humiliating. She wanted to drop through the floor, disappear from sight. How would she ever be able to explain? What would she tell him? Suddenly the revolving door incident and seeing Mr. Boggs in his underwear seemed minuscule compared to this situation. How was it that she always manages to fall into such perils?

"Lizzy, I heard you were home." Grady stepped forward. "It's good to see you."

"You too, Grady. It's been a long time." Elizabeth Anne embraced him, not a long, lingering embrace, but as if she were embracing an old friend. He returned her embrace in the same manner. "I see you have met Katherine, my daughter," she replied, pulling away.

"I have, I have indeed," Grady answered, looking back and forth, from mother to daughter. "And she's lovely, just like her mother. I don't know why I didn't see the resemblance before."

"Thank you." Little Missy kept her eyes downcast. She could not bring herself to look at him.

"You are very welcome." He bent down and whispered, "Can we finish our game later?"

Little Missy lifted her eyes, "Yes, sir."

"Good," he said, raising his voice. "Now, Lizzy, tell me all about your husband's new job. How in the world did he manage to get Hershel to agree to retirement? I figured he'd stay at the bank until his feet curled up and they had to tote him to his grave."

"Oh, Grady, you haven't changed a bit." Elizabeth Anne looped her arm through his. "Come with me, I want you to meet Benton. I've told him so much about you."

"Oh my, what stories have you told?" He pretended to resist. "What kind of fiction have you invented?" He glanced over his shoulder and winked at Little Missy.

She smiled but cautiously kept her eyes on him. He wasn't anything like she had expected, but she wasn't ready to dismiss him as harmless yet. First impressions could be deceiving.

Little Missy watched the people, still standing in clusters, nod and poke each other as her mother and Grady made their way across the crowded hardwood floor. The loud clopping sound of Grady's boots and the light tap, tap of Elizabeth Anne's open-toed pumps became louder and louder, causing everyone to stare. A hush fell upon the onlookers, they seemed to be waiting, wondering what would happen next. How would Benton Langford react?

The silence of the crowd caused Little Missy's father to turn his attention away from the judge and the mayor. He looked up, saw his wife heading in his direction and instantly realized all eyes were focused on him. He also realized the gentleman with her was undoubtedly Grady Dewberry and his reaction to this much-anticipated meeting would be the topic of discussion for days to come. He quickly waved and walked toward his wife.

Little Missy held her breath. The need to get this moment over with was weighing heavily on her. She was tempted to close her eyes, but she had to know. She, like everyone in the room, was anxious to see how her father was going to handle the situation.

Little Missy's father very cordially extended his hand. "You must be Grady," he spoke loudly. "I have been looking forward to meeting you. Elizabeth Anne has told me all about you."

Grady spoke just as loudly, "And I have been looking forward to meeting you too." He looked around the room, openly smiling at the faces staring back at him. "Since I was unable to attend your wedding years ago, please allow me to congratulate you and Lizzy on your marriage." Grady shook his hand. "And congratulations on your new job. I wish you well."

"Thank you, Grady, I appreciate your well wishes." Benton pulled his wife next to him and smiled." Let's find our table." He motioned for Grady to follow. "Let's let Grady tell us about Madam Pauline and her gypsy husband."

Elizabeth Anne's face shined with admiration for her adoring husband. He stood tall and protective next to her. She welcomed his strong arm around her, she made no effort to push him away as she had done so many times before. Her tension eased, she heaved a sigh of relief and led the way to their table. "Grady isn't as good at telling the story as I am." She smiled. "I may have to help him."

"Now, Lizzy." Grady laughed and then gave Benton a friendly slap on the back. "We all have our gifts," he said, "and mine is definitely storytelling."

Kate Carter slowly exhaled. She was grateful for the way Benton and Grady handled the embarrassing moment. She hoped their actions would finally put an end to all the whispers about Elizabeth Anne and Grady. She also hoped this night would bring an end to the rumor that Hershel was having seconds thoughts about Benton as his replacement.

She looked down at her wristwatch. Just a few more minutes, she thought to herself. A few more minutes and she would step up to the podium and repeat the speech she had carefully prepared and practiced. Ivy Holcomb had secretly told Kate that Hershel was the one responsible for starting the rumor that Benton wouldn't be able to relate to the common man. She had also told her that he had made no effort to clear out his office, not one trophy had been removed and no boxes had been packed. And she'd said that Darby Brooks was behaving more like a prima donna than ever. She had stopped hinting about wanting a raise and was now demanding one. She had stormed into Hershel's office and had threatened him, telling him that if he didn't do what he'd promised she was going to make him pay.

Neither Kate nor Ivy knew what Darby's statement meant but Kate was in agreement with the part about making Hershel pay. She simmered at his obnoxious behavior and refusal to move on. Why was he delaying? The audit was finished…weeks ago, why was he dragging his feet? Kate knew she probably would not get an answer from Hershel if she asked him but she also knew how to handle a pride-seeking, power-hungry, old coot who didn't know how to let go.

Kate plastered a smile on her face and weaved her way to the podium. She adjusted the microphone and waited until everyone was seated and then she made eye contact with Hershel Tucker.

"This night," she began, "marks the beginning of a bittersweet transition for all of us. Thomas, my dearly departed husband, and Hershel worked side-by-side from the very beginning to establish the First State Bank of Shadow Springs. Their vision of providing an honest, safe, financial institution could never have become a reality had it not been for the hard work and dedication of these two men. We have all reaped the benefits of their labor and that is why we are here tonight." Kate motioned for Hershel to stand. "Hershel, there will be no sad farewell, no long goodbye. You have unselfishly served your community and we are grateful. We appreciate you, we will miss you, but we know you are ready to move on. Your Texas ranch awaits you." Kate heightened her voice and waved her hand, emphasizing the grand finale. "We bid you God's speed, Hershel Tucker. Go, enjoy your new life and rest assured, you are leaving the bank in good hands."

Everyone stood to their feet and filled the banquet room with unrestrained applause. The board members crowded around Hershel, shaking his hand, slapping him on the back and congratulating him on a job well done. People quickly got up from their tables and formed a line. Hershel was surprised and confused. He had not expected such a jubilant sendoff. He had been prepared to deliver his long drawn-out speech, recounting his many sacrifices and his long hours of dedicated service. He had even been prepared to withdraw his resignation should the people voice their reservations about his replacement, but he had not, in his wildest dreams, anticipated an outcome such as this. He was shocked, disappointed and perturbed. He discreetly placed his speech back into his suit pocket and swore under his breath, "Sham, this is nothing but a sham."

Kate Carter took a brief moment to celebrate the fact that her plan had worked perfectly. Self-indulgent as it was, she just couldn't pass up the opportunity to delight in Hershel's dilemma. He had brought this upon himself. He should have never announced his retirement if he had no intentions of retiring. The look on his face was priceless.

Kate walked briskly to the kitchen and signaled to her staff. She wanted to start serving as soon as possible. "Travis," she pulled him to the side, "as soon as the commotion dies down, please tell the others to start with the head table. But," she looked over her shoulder, "before you do that…could you put this back in the pastor's study?" She withdrew the microphone from the folds of her dress. "We won't be needing this any more tonight." Her eyes sparkled. "Do you understand?"

"Absolutely, Mrs. Carter, I understand completely." Travis covered the microphone with a bundle of napkins and exited out the side door. When he returned he nodded.

Kate returned his nod and watched him disappear into the

kitchen then she meandered across the room to Ivy Holcomb's table. "Hope you are enjoying the festivities."

"Never enjoyed myself as much." Ivy smiled a sugary sweet smile. "Hershel looked as if his balloon popped in his face. He never saw this coming…and did you see Darby's face? She turned ghost white and then fire engine red almost at the same time." Mrs. Holcomb made no effort to hide the hint of gloating in her voice. "I guess she realized once Hershel leaves, she won't have anybody to whine to, no one to bat her eyes at. Her sweet talking days are over." She laughed aloud. "Your son-in-law is a professional. I've watched him; he isn't swayed by her womanly guiles."

"That's good to know." Kate's face lit up. "Good for you, too, no more sleepless nights worrying about Darby Brooks taking over your job. Now that she understands she's stuck as head teller she might just pack her bags and go to Texas with Hershel."

"Oh, wouldn't that be wonderful?"

"Indeed it would," Kate agreed. "Indeed it would."

Averting her eyes so she wouldn't get caught staring, Little Missy tilted her head and strained to overhear the conversation going on at the table next to her. Her father asked Grady about the mill and told him the process of spinning cotton into thread had always fascinated him.

Grady talked briefly about the different kinds of machinery but then he quickly turned the conversation in another direction. It seemed he was not interested in puffing his ego or trying to impress Benton Langford with his ability to run a cotton mill.

Little Missy's father also showed restraint. He was not interested in entering into a sparring match. He had nothing to prove. Benton did not consider himself superior. He did not boast of his intelligence. He was a man of integrity. He was determined to present himself with dignity, but his mannerisms betrayed him. He appeared stiff and standoffish, not kind, caring and loving, the way his daughter knew him to be.

Before moving to Shadow Springs, he was well respected and admired. His professionalism had been considered an asset, but now his attributes were looked down upon. He was perceived as being stuck-up and that bothered Little Missy.

She searched for some similarities between her father and Grady. Both men appeared self-confident. Benton was handsome, distinguished and sophisticated. Grady was attractive, masculine, rugged and sure. In Little Missy's eyes, the scales would have been evenly balanced had it not been for Grady's easygoing personality.

He politely greeted the people who stopped by his table, called them by their first name, and gracefully gave them an update on his mother's recent hip surgery. He repeated the story each time, without irritation, and sincerely thanked them for their concern. If only her father would relax, loosen his tie and roll up his sleeves…if only people would stop prejudging him…if only.

Little Missy sat back in her chair and forced herself to stop worrying about things she could not change. Miss Odessa had told her that worrying was good for nothing except, for producing frown lines and wrinkles.

She and Mr. Dodie had been the first to arrive at the banquet hall that morning and the last to leave that afternoon. They had worked in unison, task after task, making sure everything was perfect. They had hand washed the china, the glasses and the silverware and had carefully placed them at each table setting.

Little Missy had helped by adorning each table with a small flower-filled bud vase. "May I sit at your table tonight?" She'd asked in a dejected tone.

"We ain't gonna attend dis shindig, honey. Dis ain't no place for me and Dodie." Miss Odessa had rolled her eyes and flipped her hand back and forth. "Some folks would keel over if we was to plop ourselves down in the middle of dis banquet hall. Your heart is innocent child, but you need to understand, some folks don't see who you are…dey see who dey think you are."

"Yes ma'am, I know. James Everett thought I was unlikable because he thought I was rich."

"Yes, and some folks think dat bout me and Dodie cause we're colored. But we don't let dat bother us. We know the good Lord is colorblind. He don't care bout color."

"Me either, Miss Odessa, but…"

"But what? What's causing your face to droop like an ole hound dog?"

"I'll be the only young person here. I'm supposed to sit with Grandmother Kate, but she'll be so busy I won't have anyone to talk to."

"Who says you have to talk? Wisdom came from observing and from listening. Don't worry bout talking. Take note of your surroundings and you'll be wise and wrinkle free."

Little Missy had been hard pressed to dispute Miss Odessa's wise advice. At first, she thought she might feel self-conscious sitting alone, talking to no one, but it didn't take long for her to reap the benefits of being observant. Hearing the polite banter between her father and Grady had given her food for thought, but Darby Brooks' reaction to Grandmother Kate's speech had caused her insatiable curiosity to intensify. She struggled to come up with a logical explanation for Darby exiting the room like a whirlwind. She had scowled at Mr. Tucker and abruptly left her table without explanation, leaving her tablemates with stunned looks on their faces.

Darby's actions called for further observation, so Little Missy wrapped her fingers around her water glass, kicked off her shoes and concealed her bare feet under the long tablecloth. Despite knowing her mother would not approve, she convinced herself that such a minor detail would surely go unnoticed in a room brimming with excitement. Everyone was so absorbed in the goings-on; she could not imagine anyone shouldering the responsibility of checking to see who was wearing shoes.

Darby Brooks reentered the room, looking more poised and collected than when she left. Her tight-fitting, red dress caused many male eyes to follow her swaying hips as she paraded herself to the guest of honor's table. With her bosom pushed up and threatening to spill out, she placed her palms on the table, leaned over and spoke in a clear, loud voice, "Congratulation, Mr. Tucker, your Texas ranch awaits you." She curved her mouth into a mocking smile. "You are leaving the bank in good hands." Darby fluttered her eyelashes and stood unyielding until her resolve to over dramatize the moment was satisfied, then she prissed her way back to her table.

Mr. Tucker looked as if the wind had been knocked out of him. His expression turned from surprise to anguish and then to relief when she silently walked away.

Vivid images of a storm brewing filled Little Missy's mind as she allowed her imagination to run wild. Pictures of a scorned woman, a hanging noose and a black veil charmed her thoughts until her conscience reprimanded her for delighting in Mr. Tucker's embarrassing moment.

"Excuse me," Travis said, interrupting her thoughts. "Are you ready to be served?" He stood tall and slender. A sprinkling of freckles spread across the bridge of his nose and his cheeks were flushed. Perspiration dampened the edges of his slightly tousled, dark hair.

"Yes." She sat up, put her glass down and pushed her silverware aside.

Travis placed the food in front of her. "I'm, Travis, James Everett's brother and you're Mrs. Carter's granddaughter aren't you?"

"Yes, I am," she answered proudly.

"I remember seeing you the day we delivered Mr. Dodie's lumber."

"Yes." Little Missy felt her heart expand with compassion. "I'm sorry for the tragic death of your father. James Everett and I are trying to solve the mystery of his death."

Travis looked at her with eyes filled with concern. "My brother is high-spirited sometimes but finding Daddy the way he did has really been hard on him." His voice softened. "I appreciate you befriending him. He's convinced, and so am I, that Daddy's death was no accident."

Little Missy's stomach tightened. "I believe that, too." She nodded. "But there are so many unanswered questions." She thought long and hard, choosing her words carefully. She didn't want to offend by seemingly questioning James Everett's actions but she needed to know. "Miss Odessa said James Everett went to the sheriff's office after he found his daddy's body, why didn't he go to Mr. Tucker's house first? It was much closer."

"He did, but Mr. Tucker wasn't home." Travis looked anxious. He knew he needed to hurry; many people were waiting to be served. "The lights were on but Mr. Tucker never came to the door. James Everett drove Daddy's truck into town."

"James Everett can drive?"

"Yeah, he's been driving the tractor since he was ten years old." Travis tucked the tray under his arm and breathed deeply. His voice sounded unsure, encumbered with anxiety. "James Everett said the truck was running."

Little Missy clenched her fingers, fighting the urge to twist the hem of her dress. Her fingertips turned white. "Why would he leave his truck running if he was going to commit suicide?"

"My thoughts exactly." Travis pointed to his watch. "I've got to finish serving now, but maybe we can talk more tomorrow after church."

"Yes," Little Missy agreed. The weight of their conversation certainly warranted more discussion, much, much more.

Chapter 11

The wheels of intrigue were spinning, preoccupying Little Missy's mind for the rest of the night. She barely noticed her mother volleying her attention back and forth between her husband and Grady. She heard Nadine's constant jabber, but did not pay attention. She knew Grandmother Kate had strategically placed her at her parents' table because Nadine loved to talk. She would fill any awkward silent moments, should they arise.

After the dessert was served, the order of the evening became chaotic. Loud voices became louder. Everyone wanted to be heard, but it seemed no one wanted to listen. Hershel had attempted to find the microphone and give a final word before leaving, but no microphone was found and no final farewell was given.

Little Missy had stayed to help her grandmother oversee the clean up. She was tired and sleepy by the time they finally made it home. Her first thoughts were to go straight to bed, but as she walked past the library she heard sobs. Slowly and as quietly as possible, she cracked open the door. Her mother was curled up on the couch, her eyes were closed and tears were streaming down her face. Her head was bent backward, as if she was looking up, and she was cradling an old picture frame in her arms.

The rawness of the scene twisted at Little Missy's heart. Why, Mother, are you so sad? she asked herself silently. You looked beautiful tonight. You looked happy. You handled yourself perfectly…why? Why?

She shifted restlessly for a few moments, trying to decide if she should go in or not. What would she say to her mother? How would she comfort her? Little Missy felt helpless. She dropped her arms to her side and backed away from the doorway. "Please, God," she prayed. "Take my mother's sadness away."

The new morning light filled her bedroom. Normally, Little Missy would have sat up, shaded her eyes and basked in the beauty of her room, her castle. The lovely pink curtains, the portrait of the young girl standing in a field of flowers and her cat calendar had always brought her much delight, but not today. They only served as a reminder of how quickly time passes. The pages of the calendar had been changed several times, from the month of May, with the picture of the yellow cat and a basket of flowers, to the month of June and a picture of the cat chasing a butterfly. The month of July showed the cat playing with three balls of red, white and blue yarn. And in a few days, Little Missy would flip the page once more to reveal a new month and a picture of the cat lapping milk from a saucer.

At first, the turning of the calendar had represented a time of change, but in reality nothing had changed at all. Her life was still full of uncertainty.

The light, slicing jaggedly across her bedroom floor, reminded her of the way her heart had felt last night. The jagged edges forced her to see that no one is immune to heartache. Where love grows heartache is sure to sprout.

Little Missy decided she could not and would not spend another day without trying to expose the phantom that caused her mother's sorrow. She slipped out of bed and marched down the hall to her parent's bedroom. The door was open, the bed was unmade and the curtains were drawn.

"Mother," she called, inching her bare feet across the hard wooden floor. No answer. "Mother," she called again, her voice fading. Her determination turned into disappointment. Where is she? She wondered. It's not like her to be up so early. Little Missy's father was an early riser, but her mother liked to sleep in, especially if she'd been up late the night before.

The proper etiquette would have been for the young girl to remove herself immediately from her parent's private quarters, but she caught a glimpse of a picture frame, turned upside down on the nightstand. Was it the one her mother had clutched so tightly? Little Missy glanced in the beveled mirror hanging in front of her. The reflection showed an empty room. No one would know if she took a quick look. With shaking hands, she slowly picked up the frame and turned it over. She felt her breath catch. The picture was of her mother when she was in her early teens and a young boy. He looked about three years old. The resemblance between the two was remarkable.

Who is the little boy? Little Missy's chest tightened, her throat ached. She struggled to keep her composure. She so desperately wanted to find her mother and demand answers but she knew she had to tread lightly. Her mother was not well.

The sound of the kitchen door bursting open and banging against the back wall startled Little Missy. Her father's excited voice calling out for help, prompted her to rush into the hallway. Grandmother Kate stumbled, groggily, out of her bedroom. "What's going on?" she asked, tying her robe tightly around her waist.

Little Missy looked bewildered. "It's Father." She rushed forward and bolted down the stairs.

"Benton." Mrs. Carter followed close behind.

Mr. Doddie and Miss Odessa came out of their bedroom and crossed the hall to the parlor. "He took her in here." Mr. Doddie waved to the others. "She was limp as a dishrag."

"Oh, Lord have mercy, please sweet Jesus," Miss Odessa prayed, wringing her hands. "What has happened to our Beff Anne?"

Entering the parlor, Kate Carter clutched her chest. She was winded from running down the stairs. "What happened? Benton, is she okay?"

"Yes, the doctor gave her something to make her sleep," he answered, carefully laying his wife down on the couch. "She never came to bed, I was out all night looking for her." He stood up, his face full of worry. "I found her in the graveyard. She was distraught, I didn't know what to do." He covered her with the blanket from the back of the couch. "I finally talked her into letting me take her to the hospital."

"What was she doing in the graveyard?"

"She was lying across her brother's small grave, weeping uncontrollably."

"Her brother?" Little Missy asked, realizing she was still holding the frame. She stepped forward and held it out. "I heard Mother crying in the library last night. She was hugging this. Is this her brother?"

Reeling, Grandmother Kate took the frame. "Tommy," she whispered, her voice laced with anguish. "I thought she had gotten over his death." It was evident Mrs. Carter was trying not to cry, but despite her effort, tiny tears rolled down her cheeks. "Elizabeth Anne loved him as if he were her own. The day we brought him home she declared he was her baby. They were inseparable." She looked up, crestfallen. "She was devastated by the tragedy."

Little Missy studied the faces of the adults surrounding her. Each appeared to be injured, immersed in sorrow. Her father, a man who rarely showed his true emotions, was openly weeping. His face was drawn, his expression the saddest she had ever seen. She wanted to comfort him and she wanted to be comforted so she slipped past her grandmother and stood next to him, waiting for him to notice her. "Father," she muttered, hoping to draw his attention to her. The tremor in her voice steered his gaze downward. She felt his hand on her back, his arms pulling her close to him. His stiff and ridged body shook with grief. She pressed her head against him and locked both arms around his waist, embracing him with all her strength. She could not let go for fear she might fall. "Father, I'm scared," she whispered. "I'm scared." Pent-up tears flowed. The dam burst, there was no suppressing her feelings.

"It's going to be all right, honey." Benton promised. "Let's give her time to rest. When she wakes up, we'll talk, we'll make it better." His voice quavered. "God will get us through this."

The conversation on the way to church was almost non-existent. Little Missy sat next to her grandmother and struggled to understand why her father wouldn't answer any of her questions and why Grandmother Kate had insisted she accompany her to church. Under the circumstances, Little Missy felt she would fair just as well to stay home. The image of her father, head bowed and praying, sitting in the armchair next to his sleeping wife, and the echoing sound of the parlor door closing behind her seared into her mind like a branding iron. Her life was suspended, put on hold, confined within the walls of the parlor. Her thoughts were scattered. How could she worship when she couldn't even think straight?

The long period of silence was becoming painful. Stressful thoughts haunted Little Missy. She needed to talk so she blurted out her grandmother's name.

Grandmother Kate jumped. "What, sweetie?"

"Tell me about Tommy. How did he die?"

"My sweet, precious baby drowned, but I can't talk about it right now." She blinked repeatedly and summoned her resolved. "I can't relive that tragedy now…not on my way to church."

"Why are we going to church?"

"Because, honey." Mrs. Carter cut her eyes toward her granddaughter. "We have to keep up appearances. We can't let folks see our pain. There is too much gossip already. We don't need to fuel the fire."

Little Missy turned sideways. "My eyes are swollen. Everyone will know I've been crying."

"Kate Carter rifled through her handbag and pulled out a small cosmetic case. "Here, powder your face."

"Make up?"

"Just a little, don't over do." Mrs. Carter gripped the steering wheel and turned her eyes back to the road. "We should be very discreet when we get to church. We shouldn't mention your mother's state of mind." She lowered her voice. Her eyebrows dipped, her lips pulled tight with determination. "Do you know how to play-act?"

"Pretend?"

"Yes, can you pretend that you don't have a care in the world? Can you act as if nothing is bothering you?"

"Yes, ma'am, I think so."

"Good, let's show everyone what we're made of, okay?"

"What do you mean?"

"I want you to put all your worries aside until we get back home. Don't say anything to anyone." Grandmother Kate took a deep breath and forced a smile. "The strength and character of a woman has always been determined by her ability to portray strength and character. Do you understand?"

Little Missy nodded. She wasn't sure she fully understood, but she did understand enough to know that her grandmother's words were words of wisdom.

The church service was spirit-filled, the sermon about hellfire and brimstone was attention grabbing, but Little Missy thought her faked, plastered on smile would surely crack and fall off her face before the preacher decided it was time to dismiss. She had hidden her despair, the best she could, by honing all of her attention on what the preacher was saying, but his closing prayer seemed endless, so much so, that she gave in to the temptation to open her eyes. She looked around. James Everett and his family sat in their usual pew, but Travis was sitting near the front with Peggy Shaddix, the pastor's daughter. Grady Dewberry, his first time to attend since his mother's fall, had the misfortune of being wedged between Nadine and Ivy Holcomb. Poor soul, Little Missy thought. He's probably as anxious as I am to hear the pastor say amen.

Finally, the prayer ended and the congregation filed out into the aisles. Little Missy followed her grandmother and watched her give a performance worthy of a movie star. She smiled and convincingly portrayed the southern matriarch role as if her heart was being softly caressed with velvet instead of being harshly rubbed with sandpaper. She gracefully and humbly accepted the barrage of praise and accolades for Mr. Tucker's retirement party. She was dignified and refined in her reaction to Charlotte Wilkes and Florence Digby when they stuck their noses up and walked past as if they were deaf, dumb and blind. Mrs. Carter simply adverted her eyes away from the old biddies and smiled sweetly.

James Everett pushed forward. "Travis asked me to tell you that he won't be able to talk today, he's going to eat lunch with Peggy."

"That's okay, I need to hurry home anyway." Little Missy looked around, making sure no one could hear. She whispered, "When are we planning to go back to Miss Ella's?"

"Anytime you want to, why?"

"I've been thinking…she said your father told her he had found what he was looking for and he had hidden it. Do you think he hid it at her house or on her property? She's blind…it could be in plain sight…she wouldn't know."

"I ain't thought about that." His eyes brightened. "We could go tomorrow."

She nodded. "I'll be ready as soon as I finish my chores."

With her plans set for tomorrow, Little Missy decided to wait in the car for her grandmother. Her stomach was churning. She wasn't as good at pretending as Grandmother Kate, she was nervous and fidgety. She wanted to hurry home. She needed answers.

Kate Carter quickly opened the car door and slid inside. "Sorry, I couldn't get away faster, the preacher's wife stopped me. She asked me to return this to Darby." She held up a red shawl. "She said Darby left it in the banquet room last night."

Little Missy's eyes widened. "She certainly wasn't wearing a shawl when I saw her." She made a face. "It reeks of perfume…it…" She stopped. "It reeks of A Joyful Rose."

"Yes, it does. Darby Brooks has expensive taste, but evidently she doesn't know perfume is to be used in moderation. Too much of a good thing is just that-too much."

Little Missy didn't comment. Her mind was racing. She couldn't wait to tell James Everett. This had to be more than a coincidence.

Chapter 12

It was late in the afternoon before the sedative wore off. Elizabeth Anne refused food, but Benton had persuaded her to drink a little warm tea. She reluctantly accepted the cup, took a few sips and placed it on the side table.

"Are you ready to talk now?" Benton asked. His voice was soft and affectionate.

Elizabeth Anne looked up and gave a slight nod. He laid a comforting hand on her shoulder and stared down at her worried face. He ached for her; he wished he could take away her pain.

His wife reached up, squeezed his hand, then unclasped it and nodded again. "This is like a scab that won't heal. I can't go on like this." The color was gone from her face. Her voice was weak. She hedged. "I can't delude myself any longer. I have to do this."

"Yes, I agree." Benton walked to the door and quickly opened it. He didn't hesitate; he didn't want to give his wife time to change her mind. "She's ready now," he announced.

Grandmother Kate, Little Missy, Mr. Dodie and Miss Odessa entered the parlor together. They followed Benton to the chairs he had placed in a semi-circle around the couch. He sat next to his wife and put his arm around her. "Elizabeth Anna has something she needs to say." He cleared his throat. His eyes reflected deep pain and sorrow. "I promised her we would all listen."

She turned from her husband and looked toward the caring faces staring back at her. "I'm sorry." Her voice was barely audible. She dropped her gaze. "I'm sorry, I..." she slowly lifted her eyes and took a deep breath. "I try to make the hurt go away, but no matter what I do, it always comes back." Her voice trembled. "Guilt attacks me each time I smile or feel the least bit happy." Elizabeth Anne burst into tears. "God is punishing me." She covered her face with her hands.

"Honey, no." Benton pulled her close. "God isn't punishing you. You've done nothing to…"

"Yes, He is, Benton." She pushed him away. "You don't understand. God took away our baby. He knows I don't deserve to be happy."

Kate Carter reached for her daughter.

"No mother, don't." Elizabeth Anne threw up her hands. "Don't touch me, don't try to comfort me."

"But sweetie," she withdrew her hand, "why do you think God is punishing you? Why do you think you don't deserve to be happy?"

"Mother, you know…" She choked back the tears. "Tommy, it was my fault he drown."

"No, honey, no."

"Yes, Mother. It was my fault and that's why God took away my baby. I was going to name him Tommy. I was going to…I was going to…" She contorted her face, trying to fight back the tears. "But God took him, too." Elizabeth Anne looked at her husband. "He took our son and it's all my fault."

"Darling." Benton reached out.

"No, please." Elizabeth Anne blocked him. "I don't deserve your pity. I've asked God to take me, too, so I won't cause any more pain."

"Miss Beff Anne, you stop talking like that." Mr. Dodie sprang up from his seat. "You was no where around when young Tommy fell in the well. I seen you leave with your friends."

Miss Odessa yanked at his shirt and shook her head. "She's upset, don't make it worse," she warned.

Mr. Dodie calmed his voice and said, "I'm sorry Miss Beff Anne, I don't mean to get all rowdy, but I jest can't let you blame yourself for something you ain't guilty of."

"Oh, Dodie, you've always been the first one to come to my rescue." Elizabeth Anne pulled the blanket close to her chest. "You've always been my protector, but you can't protect me from this." She reached up, smoothed down her hair and gave a weak smile. "I remember that day, as a matter of fact, I've relived it so many times it has become a nightmare." She leaned her head back against the cushion. "It was the prettiest of summer days. The sun was bright yellow, the sky was robin's egg blue and the sweet smell of magnolia filled the air. I was waiting on the front porch for Becky and Joyce and Caroline. We were all going to ride our bicycles into town and go to the movies, but little Tommy was anxious to go water the calf." She looked at her mother. "Do you remember the calf daddy bought from Mr. Forsyth?"

Her mother nodded.

"Tommy always looked forward to helping me. Every afternoon he'd run and get his little bucket and tell me he was a big boy, then he'd grab my hand and lead the way to the well." She smiled at his memory. "I'd let him help me wind the rope handle and pour the water into his bucket but I never let him unlatch the well cover, I promise, I never did." She rapidly shook her head. "I knew it was too dangerous. I always made him stand back so he couldn't see how to unlatch it, but somehow he knew…he figured it out and…and." Elizabeth Anne clenched her hands, her mouth strained to form the words, but they did not come. She took a long pause to gather her strength and then slowly she began again. "I…I explained it was too early. I told him he could help me when I got back, but he started to cry." She raised her pitch, imitating her baby brother's voice. "'I big boy. I can do it, Sissy,' he said. 'I can do it by myself.' I told him no… that he had to wait until I got back. But when we were riding off, I heard him call, 'I big boy, Sissy.'" Elizabeth Anne threw off the blanket and stood up. "I knew within my heart, I shouldn't leave him…I heard that warning voice in my mind, telling me not to go---But I did! I rode off with my friends---and when I came back home and found out that he was missing…I knew, I knew where he was.

The desperate, sad, lonely sound of Mother's voice calling for him was like a hard blow to my stomach. I grabbed my ears. I didn't want to hear his name. I didn't want to remember his tiny voice saying, 'I big boy, Sissy.' My heart ached as I stumbled to the well. I dreaded each step, I dreaded what I would see…and when I got there…the cover had been pushed to the side, the bucket was hanging high; it had not been lowered. In my mind I could see little Tommy reaching for it, getting off balance and falling. Oh, dear Lord, not my sweet Tommy, I begged. Please, God, not Tommy! But it was…his little hands spread wide…he was face down, floating on top of the water. He was dead, he drown in the well!" Her shoulders slumped. Tears rolled down her cheeks "Oh, God, in heaven, please forgive me…his death is my fault. I could have saved him if only…if only I had stayed."

Unable to stop herself, Little Missy jumped up and threw her arms around her mother's waist. She couldn't bare the agony. Her mother's intense suffering wrenched her soul. She felt powerless to do anything, but to cling to her and beg her to stop crying. "Please, Mother, don't cry. It's not your fault, it's not."

Elizabeth Anne relaxed her body and wrapped her arms around her daughter, embracing her with her last ounce of strength. Benton stood, too, and interlocked them both, comforting them, soothing them, giving them stability.

Katherine Carter waited a short period and then she gently pried between them. "Elizabeth Anne, why didn't you tell me you felt this way. I could have saved you so much sorrow." She motioned for them to sit down. "Dodie took Tommy to water the calf. It wasn't your fault."

"Dats right, Miss Beff Anne." Mr. Dodie spoke up. "Young Tommy helped Odessa hang out the clothes and then she brought him to me. He looked so cute with his big grin and his little water bucket dat he melted my heart. I jest couldn't make him wait."

"He's telling the truth." Miss Odessa nodded. "After you and your friends left, he come a running to the clothes line. He wanted to help so I let him hand me the clothes, one piece at a time, and then we went and found Dodie at the woodpile."

"And after we watered the calf we came back to the house and ate lunch." Mr. Dodie shook his head. "Poor little feller was so tuckered out he fell asleep at the table." He looked straight into Elizabeth Anne's eyes. "I helped Missus Kate put him down for a nap. He was sound asleep, looked like a little angel when we left his room."

"Is that true?" Elizabeth Anne asked, looking at her mother. "You're not making that up to…to take away my guilt?"

"We would never do that," Kate Carter assured her daughter. "And you're not guilty of anything. At first, I wanted to blame myself too, for not watching him closer, for not hearing him when he got out of bed, for not knowing he went outside. Thomas did the same thing. He cursed the day he bought the calf, but finally, after much prayer, we both realized that no one is to blame. God allowed us to have Tommy for a short time and that time, no matter how short, was a blessing. He brought so much love into our lives."

"Why did he go to the well?" Elizabeth Anne searched for answers.

"I don't know." Kate shook her head. "I've asked myself that a million times."

Little Missy remembered Miss Odessa telling her that the Bible speaks of secret things belonging to God. She spoke up. "Some things are not for us to understand. God doesn't expect us to know the answers to everything." She looked at Miss Odessa. "Isn't that right?"

"It sho is, child," she answered. "It sho is."

Chapter 13

"It was inarguably the worst night I've ever experienced," Elizabeth Anne stated as she sat at the kitchen table. Her hair hung loosely around her neck. Her face was blotchy and her eyes were swollen. "Poor Benton didn't get much sleep either, but I think I've finally come to terms with my torment. I'm determined to stop chastising myself for the past and allow God to ease my pain."

"I'm glad you were able to get everything out in the open. It's time to heal." Kate Carter met her daughter's gaze. "I had two miscarriages before Tommy was born. With each loss my heart sank lower and lower but Tommy's death hit so hard, I thought I would never recover. And when your father died I questioned God. I questioned my ability to overcome but somehow…little by little, day by day, I found the strength to go on, and you will too," her mother promised.

Little Missy heard muffled voices, so she held her breath and waited before entering the kitchen. Once she realized her mother and grandmother were having a private conversation, she retraced her steps to the dining room. The hired hands had finished eating and Miss Odessa was busy clearing the table.

"May I have a biscuit?" she asked. "I haven't had breakfast yet and James Everett will be here in a few minutes. I'll wait for him on the porch."

"You getting started early, ain't you?" Miss Odessa broke open a biscuit and placed a warm slice of fried ham inside. "I seen you doing your chores while I was cooking breakfast this morning. What are you and James Everett up to?" Her voice was sprinkled with suspicion. "Y'all ain't thinking bout going back to the Richardson Estate, are you?" Her eyebrows shot up. "I heard bout y'all being there from Miss Beff Anne. She said y'all looked guiltier than a bear caught with a honey jar. What was y'all looking for?" She smiled a big smile. "Wasn't a dead body and a golden candlestick was it?"

"Yes, ma'am it was." Little Missy twisted her mouth. "But there was no parlor and we didn't see anything that look remotely like a dead body."

"So y'all plan to go back?"

"Not today." Little Missy took a big bite of the biscuit. "We're concentrating on another mystery. We're fixing our attention on Mr. Holloway's killer."

"Killer. Did you say killer?" Her words sounded abrupt and troubled. "What are you young'uns up to?"

"Oh, nothing, Miss Odessa." Little Missy peered up at her and slowly stepped toward the back porch. "We're just putting our heads together with Miss Ella to see if we can figure out what really happened to Mr. Wiley."

"You wait a minute, young lady," Miss Odessa ordered. She crossed her arms and stared in a way that meant she wasn't going to put up with foolishness. "It ain't escaped my notice dat you have a curious streak," she cocked her head to the side, "and I'm here to remind you dat curiosity killed the cat."

"Yes, ma'am." Little Missy nodded. She was relieved to hear James Everett coming up the back steps. "I'll remember that. Yes, ma'am, I surely will," she shouted and out the door she fled.

"What you hollering about?" James Everett asked.

"Oh, nothing." Little Missy shifted her biscuit to her left hand and picked up the bag on the small wicker table.

"What's that?"

"Miss Ella's package from me. It's toothpaste, toothbrush, soap, some sweet smelling perfume, a hair brush and some hair clips."

"Why are you giving her that stuff?"

"Because I think she would like to have them." She stretched her neck forward. "Here, smell...don't I smell nice?"

James Everett backed up. "I ain't gonna smell you," he wrinkled his nose, "and Miss Ella ain't gonna want that junk. She can't eat primping stuff."

"James Everett Holloway, you do know how to darken a bright

sunny day. I truly believe you are the most negative person I've ever met."

"I ain't negative, just using common sense. What's a blind woman gonna do after she gets all primped up? Look in the mirror?"

Little Missy squinted her eyes and fixed her jaw. "She's going to feel beautiful and she is going to smell pretty and she is going to think to herself that you could benefit from more personal grooming as well." She tucked the bag under her arm and marched down the steps.

"Are you saying I stink? Is that what you're saying?"

"I would never be so rude, but…I do intend to stay down wind from you," she said loudly without looking back. She led the way down the path, eating her biscuit as she went. She stayed in the lead until she got to the railroad tracks, then she stopped to listen for a train. "You hear anything?"

"No, but that don't mean nothing. The train don't run on a schedule. We still have to be careful."

Little Missy agreed and fell into step with James Everett. They walked side by side until they came to the trestle and then he pointed to the big rock extending out and over the water below. Part of the rock was embedded into the bank but a long, wide ledge hung over the creek, providing the perfect spot for sunbathers. "That looks like Sadie."

"Your sister?"

"Yeah, and her friends, Donna Jo and Carrie. I wonder what they're doing here." He looked worried. "Let's go find out."

The bank leading to the water was steep and difficult. There were lots of rocks and potholes covered by the tall grass. Their footing was unsure. It was hard to stay upright so Little Missy and James Everett stopped halfway down.

"What are y'all doing?" James Everett called to his sister from the other side of the creek. "Does Mama know you're here?"

"Yeah, Mrs. Wilkes was having one of her headaches. She sent Mama home early." Sadie stood up. "We're having a picnic. Do y'all want to join us?"

"Naw, we gotta go." James Everett turned quickly, obviously not interested in picnicking with his sister and her friends. But Little Missy lingered. She would have loved to join the girls. She wanted to call out to them, tell them she wanted to be their friend, but she couldn't find the courage. Instead, she waved and slowly made her way up the bank. James Everett was just about to step up on the tracks when sudden there was a terrible rumbling sound. The ground began to shake.

"A train is coming!" he shouted and jumped down the bank. He ran toward Little Missy and forced her to drop to her knees. They were only a few feet from the tracks but from their viewpoint they could see underneath the train as it traveled over the squealing rails. The crossties wobbled from side to side, forming a large cloud of dust. The wooden supports creaked, moaned and groaned.

"Oh, my goodness." Little Missy covered her ears and waited until the caboose went by. "That was so quick. Are you okay?"

James Everett looked around. "Yeah, are you?"

"Yes."

He stood up. The dust cloud was drifting downward. He called to Sadie, "Y'all okay?"

The girls waved and fanned the dust away and then they gathered their things and moved off the rock.

Little Missy grabbed Miss Ella's bag and struggled her way up the hill.

"That was scary. I'm so glad we weren't on the trestle." She wiped her face with the back of her hand.

"Me too." James Everett took a deep breath and let it out slowly. "We would have had no place to go."

Little Missy ran and rang the dinner bell. "Miss Ella, Miss Ella," she shouted as she approached the porch. James Everett rolled his eyes. He was accustomed to waiting for Miss Ella to come out before approaching the house, but his friend was already banging on the front door. She barely allowed the door to crack open before barging in and announcing she had a special package.

The old lady genuinely seemed pleased with all the things in the bag. She felt each gift and smelled the perfume over and over. Her excitement resembled that of a young child at Christmas. She allowed Little Missy to brush her hair and pin it back with a pearl clip. "I've never received such a thoughtful gift. Thank you," she softly whispered. "No one has ever tried to make me pretty, except my mother and," she dropped her head, "that was such a long time ago."

As much as James Everett hated to admit it, it seemed Little Missy had been right. Miss Ella transformed from a duckling into a swan before his very eyes. He stepped back and took a quick whiff under his arms. His discovery disturbed him…he did, indeed, need to devote more time on his daily hygiene. "Didn't we come here to talk about something else?" he asked, hoping to steer the conversation in another direction.

"Yes," Little Missy answered, picking up the bag. "I brought this too," she pulled out the red shawl. "Darby Brooks left it at Mr. Tucker's retirement party and it smells just like the handkerchief. Smell." She passed it around. "A Joyful Rose, there's no denying it."

"You're right," Miss Ella agreed. "But who is Darby Brooks?"

"She's the head teller at the bank." James Everett answered with a tone of enlightenment. "That would make sense. If Mr. Tucker is involved in some wrongdoing, if he had anything to do with daddy's death, then she could be involved too or at least, she might know something."

"That's exactly what I thought." Little Missy grinned. "So after we finish here, I thought you and I would walk into town and return this to Miss Brooks."

James Everett looked confused. "Why?"

"Because I have a few questions I want to ask her." She held up her hands, to ward off any negative protest he might have. "I'm not going to accuse her of anything. I just want to gather some information."

"See, James Everett," Miss Ella spoke up. "I told you we would benefit by letting Little Missy help us. I think she is on the right path."

"Yeah, maybe." He thought for a moment. "Daddy told you he hid something…do you think he hid it on your property?"

Miss Ella's blind stare softened. "It could be…I heard him drive up, but he didn't ring the bell right away. He could have had time to hide it, whatever it was."

"Do you mind if we search your property?"

"No, please do. Your daddy was a kind person; he worked hard to overcome his thorn in the flesh. He deserves to have justice."

The children spent the rest of the morning searching for the elusive prize. The shed, the outhouse, the well, the woodpile revealed nothing. Miss Ella was disappointed and so were Little Missy and James Everett. As they walked into town, they talked about the next most logical place to look…Mr. Tucker's barn.

"Maybe we can figure out a way to get into the barn without getting caught," Little Missy said. "While we're at the bank we can pump Mrs. Holcomb for information about Mr. Tucker. See if she knows when he'll be moving his things out of his office. We could sneak out to his farm while he's in town."

"Yeah, sounds good." James Everett's mind started to drift. They were no closer to solving the mystery, no progress had been made today and they were pretty much right back where they'd started. "What information are you after with Darby Brooks? What questions are you gonna ask her?"

"I don't know," Little Missy admitted. "I really just want to return her shawl and watch her reaction. She behaved strangely at the retirement party, as if she has something against Mr. Tucker."

"Like a grudge?"

"No, more like she knows some kind of secret and if he doesn't do what she wants, she will tell."

"What could she know?"

"I don't know," Little Missy confessed, "but we can't get sidetracked by what we don't know."

"You can say that again," James Everett joked, "because at this point we don't know more than we do know."

"You're confusing me," Little Missy answered in a lighthearted way. "But there is one thing I do know." she looked at him sideways. "I know I'm about to starve." She smiled and patted her pocket. "I have money. We could stop at Cecil's Café." She poked him with her elbow. "Race you the rest of the way to town."

"I don't need your money." James Everett grabbed her by her arms and spun her around. He quickly sidestepped her and took off as fast as he could. "Looser buys lunch," he yelled.

"You cheated," she yelled back.

Little Missy sprinted forward and ran until the pain in her side forced her to stop. She walked a little and ran a little until she caught up with James Everett. He was sitting on the ground across from the main gate of the Richardson Estate.

"You big cheat," she huffed.

"You slow poke," he teased.

"It's way too hot to run." Little Missy sat down next to him.

"The race was your idea, remember." He laughed and ran his hand through his hair.

"Yeah, I remember." She looked across the road and pouted her lips. "Look at that big monster." She pulled her knees up to her chest and wrapped her arms around her legs. "The house is so close to the bank, Father could surely walk to work."

"Do you think he's gonna buy it?"

"I don't know." Her eyes followed the long drive up the hill to the circular driveway. The front of the mansion was much more impressive than the back. The large white columns were two stories high. The porch ran the full length of the house and a set of wide brick steps fanned out from the middle like a pair of welcoming arms.

James Everett nudged her. "There are worse things than living in a place like that."

"She nudged him back and smiled. "Yes, like having to buy lunch."

The inside of the café was cooler that the outside, but not by much. Little Missy and James Everett quickly scooted into the nearest booth and ordered lunch.

"It's going to take a few minutes," the young waitress told them. She smiled sweetly and slipped her pad inside her apron pocket. "Isn't Travis Holloway you're brother?"

James Everett nodded.

"He's very cute," she whispered softly. "My name is Lilly. Is he going to be joining you?" She twisted her body and put her hands on her hips.

"No." James Everett tilted his head and looked up at her. He waited for her to move, but she stood still, making no effort to place their order.

"He's not going to stop by today." She frowned. "It's been several days now." Lilly looked around the room, making sure Cecil wasn't scowling at her from behind the counter. "Will you tell Travis I said hello?"

James Everett was hungry. His stomach was growling louder than a grouchy old man. "Yeah, sure." He stared at her blankly and wondered why his brother's whereabouts was so important. "Yeah, I'll tell him," he repeated.

"Thank you." The waitress did a quick curtsey and scurried off to the kitchen.

Little Missy giggled and turned to look out the window. Carter's Mill was directly across the street. Some employees were standing under the awning at the side of the building and some were sitting on the steps, eating their lunch. Brown paper bags set beside them.

The red brick building was impressive. The sign above the front entrance noted the establishment date as 1908. Little Missy suddenly felt a sense of pride. She was in awe that the mill had been in her family for almost 50 years. She tried to imagine the machines, the looms and the process of spinning cotton into thread. She wished she and her grandmother had gone inside that day.

"Hey, aren't you hungry?" James Everett's words brought her back to the present. The waitress had delivered their food and was now taking the orders of the people two booths away.

James Everett bowed his head, asked the blessing and then he picked up his burger with both hands and took a big bite. "Mmmm, good." He grinned.

Little Missy returned his grin and took a big bite, too. She did not take the time to slice her hamburger in two or spread her napkin across her lap. She didn't concern herself with the grease running down her wrist or the catsup oozing out the sides of her mouth. She was hungry and the food was delicious.

They sat in silence until the meal was over then James Everett quickly picked up his ticket. "I pay my own way," he stated proudly. "Travis pays me for helping him. He says it's the right thing to do. He says we are to earn our keep, pay our tithes and be responsible for our debts."

Little Missy didn't try to argue or insist that she had lost the bet. He was the faster runner, but winning the race wasn't the issue. His pride was. She knew it would embarrass him if she paid for his meal, so they each paid separately.

"Now, let's return this to Darby." She held up the shawl and turned to leave but before she got to the door she noticed Grady Dewberry sitting at the corner booth. He looked up and waved to her. She waved back, not intending to stop and make conversation, but she noticed a very attractive lady sitting beside him. Her curiosity peaked. "Let's go say hello," she said, pushing James Everett forward.

"Well, hello there," Grady greeted them with a smile. "I didn't expect to see y'all here. How are you Katherine? How are you James Everett?"

"I'm fine, sir." James Everett nodded.

"Me, too," Little Missy answered politely. "We're on our way to the bank." She turned toward the lady and waited for an introduction.

"This is Leola." Grady touched her arm gently. "She was my mother's nurse when she was in the hospital in Atlanta."

"I used to live in Atlanta." Little Missy's eyes lit up. "But I live here now."

"Is that so?" Leola smiled. "Grady has been showing me around. I like your lovely town."

Little Missy's inquisitive nature took over. Was Grady interested in his mother's former nurse in a way other than friendship? Did she feel the same way? "Are you thinking about moving here?" she asked.

"Just here for a visit today." Leola took a sip from her tea glass. "He gave me a tour of the mill." She covered her ears in a mocking fashion. "Too loud."

Grady laughed and then he asked Little Missy, "Did the person you were looking for at the retirement party ever show up?"

She thought hard and chose her words carefully. "No, sir, the person I expected did not show up, but that's okay, because I met someone a lot nicer."

"Good," Grady responded. "Please thank your grandmother for inviting me."

"I will," Little Missy said as she walked away. She felt as if her burden had been lightened, some of her stress had diminished. Her mother seemed to be on the road to recovery, Grady Dewberry was totally opposite from the person she had perceived him to be and Mr. Tucker was finally going to leave the bank. Things were beginning to look up.

Chapter 14

The bank was crowded for a Monday afternoon. All the tellers were busy, so the children stood patiently in Darby Brooks' line. Little Missy took out the shawl, folded the bag and then handed it to James Everett. "Here, see if you can put this in your pocket. We don't want anybody to think we're going to rob the bank."

"Nobody is going to think that." He made a face and shook his head. "Two kids robbing the bank…imagine that."

"Oh, hush up, your sarcasm isn't needed."

"And neither is your wild imagination." James Everett stepped out of line. "I'm going to wait over yonder." He pointed to the bench against the wall. "I don't want to chance being mistaken for a criminal."

Little Missy clamped her lips together to keep from saying something she would regret. He was impossible to get along with. The sight of him meandering toward the bench, smiling at her from across the room made her mad. She fought the urge to remind him that she was trying to collect information, uncover some clues that might aide them in solving his father's mystery. She was on a mission and his attitude certainly wasn't helping.

One by one the line got shorter. Little Missy was next in line behind a tall gentleman wearing an old pair of dirty overalls and a red ball cap. His face was tanned from years of working in the sun and lined with deep wrinkles. He held a worn notebook in his callused hands.

When it became his turn, he stomped up to the counter, slammed down his notebook and pulled out an envelope from his bib pocket. He seemed a little nervous at first but within a few minutes his nervousness turned into anger. His voice became sharp and loud. "You ain't telling me nothing, young lady," he yelled. "I'm telling you that

I ain't behind in my payments. I've always paid on time and you or nobody in this here bank is gonna foreclose on my property."

"Mr. Phillips, Mr. Phillips." Darby tried to calm him. She hurried around the counter and took him by the elbow. "Let's go into the conference room. I can explain, sir."

He yanked his arm away. "I ain't going nowhere with you. You get Hershel out here. I aim to see Hershel Tucker." He turned around in such a hurry he almost ran over Little Missy. He shot her an angry look. His face was fiery red, the veins in his forehead were bulging and his nostrils were flared. His rage-filled stare startled her.

"I'm sorry sir," she said quickly stepping back.

He grunted and swatted the air with the back of his hand. "Hershel Tucker, you git yoself out here rat now," he shouted, stretching his neck.

James Everett ran to Little Missy's side and grabbed her shoulders. They swapped bewildered looks.

"Mr. Tucker isn't here." Darby shushed him. She looked around. Every person in the bank was staring. "Hershel has retired, Mr. Phillips. Please calm down and come with me." She cautiously extended her hand toward him, careful not to touch him. "You're causing a commotion."

"I mean to cause a fuss, that's why I'm here." Mr. Phillips lifted his hand and shook the envelope. "Y'all see this here letter?" He turned back toward the tellers. "It says that my farm ain't mine. It says it belongs to the bank. This letter is a lie. Nothing but a lie." He turned again and pointed his finger toward Darby. "You and every one of them tellers know I come in here every month. I pay my payment on time, I ain't never late and then I git this here…" He crushed the envelope and threw it in Darby's face. "Little lady, you best be gittin Hershel out here rat now!"

"Mr. Tucker isn't here." Little Missy's father spoke loud and clear. He walked out from his office with his hand extended. "I'm Benton Langford, the new bank president." He held his head high, his shoulders straight. "Sir, I understand you being upset. I would be, too." He reached out and firmly gripped Mr. Phillips' hand. "I'm sure this is just a minor discrepancy, come on into my office and we'll sit down, man-to-man, and figure this out."

"This ain't no minor nothing and I don't need no highfaluting, suit wearing, con man out here trying to swindle me out of what's rightfully mine."

"No sir, you certainly don't." Benton pointed to the notebook. "I see you brought your ledger." He looked at Darby. "Get Mr. ah…"

"Melvin Phillips," she said.

"Yes, get Melvin's file and bring it into my office." Benton put his arm around the older man's shoulder. "Give me a few minutes of your time, Melvin. I'm sure we'll be able to straighten out any discrepancies."

Mr. Phillips relaxed. He looked around at the onlookers and lowered his eyes. "It wasn't my intention to stir up no trouble," he spoke softly. "I just wanted to git this thang worked out."

"No trouble at all, I admire a man who is straightforward," Benton answered loudly.

Little Missy and James Everett stood in the middle of the room and waited for everybody to go back to what they were doing. Darby Brooks retrieved the requested file and disappeared into the president's office.

"What do we do now?" Little Missy asked. "Father didn't see us, Darby Brooks is unavailable and I don't know where Mrs. Holcomb is." She pitched the red shawl to James Everett. "It doesn't look as if we're going to be able to do what we came here to do."

"So what am I supposed to do with this?" He pitched it back.

"I don't know." She shrugged. "Should we leave it at her counter or should we wait for her to return?"

"Just leave it," James Everett answered. He picked up the crumpled letter, smoothed it out and sighed. His frustration was evident.

"What's wrong?" Little Missy asked.

"I thought we were the only ones who got one of these letters. Mr. Phillips and…I wonder who else."

"Oh," Little Missy said. "I see."

"Do you think I should talk to your daddy too?" James Everett was eager for answers. "Do you think he will meet with me and Travis?"

"Yes," she answered. "I know he will."

"Let's go see if we can find Travis, I think he's painting the back steps at Doc Whatley's clinic."

Little Missy placed the shawl on Darby's counter and she and James Everett hurried to the clinic. A wet paint sign hung on the steps hand railing but no Travis. The nurse said they had just missed him.

"So what now?" Little Missy blotted the perspiration off her forehead. "It's too hot to be running all over town."

"Yeah, I guess we'll go home." James Everett ran his fingers through his hair. "Maybe me and Travis can talk to your daddy tomorrow." He led the way back down the street, but before they got to the bank he changed directions. "This way is shorter," he said, darting between the Piggly Wiggly and the hardware store. The tall buildings blocked the sun, casting a cool shadow across the grassy area leading to the bank's back parking lot.

"Oh, sweet relief," Little Missy sighed. She stopped briefly to catch her breath and to indulge in the shade. The stifling afternoon sun was almost unbearable. How could James Everett stand the hot pavement on his bare feet? She would have loved to remove her shoes and wiggle her toes in the coolness of the grass, but she knew she would surely be left behind if she did. James Everett was several feet ahead and didn't appear to be slowing down, so she did a quick sprint in order to catch up with him. "Why do you always walk so fast?" she asked, pulling at his arm. She hoped to slow him down but didn't expect him to come to a complete halt. Her chin slammed into the back of his head. "What…"

"Shhh." James Everett grabbed her and pulled her with him to the side of the building. "Shhh." He nodded toward the parking lot. "It's Darby and Mr. Tucker."

Mr. Tucker was standing next to his truck with the door open. It looked as if he had just stepped out. Darby was facing him, waving her arms and motioning with her hands. They were too far away to hear what she was saying, but she seemed excited and from the expression on Mr. Tucker's face he was excited, too.

"I bet she's telling him about Mr. Phillips." James Everett slowly released his grip.

"Do you think she is warning him, telling him not to go inside?" whispered Little Missy.

"Probably, looks like he's leaving."

Chapter 15

James Everett and Travis did meet with Benton Langford and so did several other families from across the county. Mr. Phillips' tirade caused more and more families to come forward. The number of farms being foreclosed on swelled higher and higher and it didn't seem to matter if their payments were current or not, the letters kept coming. Speculations on who might be next were so rampant that folks were hesitant to go to the post office for fear they too, might receive foreclosure papers.

Almost everybody was in an uproar about the way the new bank president was handling the situation. They said he was hard and unsympathetic. They accused him of being too sophisticated to take into account the struggles of poor folks and they said they were tired of him telling them that the matter was being investigated. They wanted answers and they wanted them now.

The board of directors cowered down to the demands of the angry mob by calling a special meeting, but unfortunately, the meeting accomplished nothing except to provide an occasion to swap insults and accusations. The majority of the board members placed the blame on Benton Langford. Nothing like this had ever happened when Hershel Tucker was in charge, so the only logical explanation was that it was Benton's fault.

Clovis Daniels, the board president, insisted Sheriff Connelly attend the meeting to make sure it was conducted in an orderly manner, but halfway through, he boldly stood up and presented a motion to have Mr. Langford arrested.

"This whole mess has been going on a lot longer than the time Mr. Langford has been the president," the sheriff told them while standing at the head of the long conference table. "I can't arrest somebody because y'all don't think he fits in." He looked up and down both sides of the table and asked, "Where is Hershel?"

The absence of Hershel Tucker was explained by the fact that he had left soon after his retirement party to go to Texas. He was making final arrangements for the move to his new ranch. Darby Brooks had been able to reach him by phone and had made him aware of the mayhem the good citizens of Shadow Springs were enduring. He had promised to straighten everything out the minute he got back into town.

"Then, that's exactly what I suggest y'all do." Sheriff Connelly said. "Have Hershel come see me when he gets back, but until then, let Mr. Langford do his job. I was in his office when he called Neville Boggs. The State Auditor and the FBI are investigating this so I suggest y'all go home and keep your mouths shut. I see no sense in stirring up more trouble."

The sheriff's attitude did not sit well with the board members. They reminded him that he was an elected official and come the next election, he might find himself without a job. Sheriff Connelly, in turn, reminded them that as long as he was the sheriff, he would uphold the law, even if it meant hauling every last one of them off to jail.

The heated outburst ruffled a lot of feathers and caused Pastor Clifford Shaddix so much concern that he felt compelled to preach his next sermon on brotherly love. He stepped up to the pulpit, laid his Bible down, raised his hands and quoted the scriptures, "The mouth of a righteous man is a well of life, but violence covereth the mouth of the wicked. Hatred stirreth up strife, but love covereth all sins."

As Little Missy sat in church with her family, she held her head high and wore her plastered-on smile with determination and pride. Grandmother Kate's lesson on play-acting and keeping up appearances proved to be valuable, not only in church but also in the day to day business of living. Going to the grocery store or going into the bank was harder than a camel trying to go through the eye of a needle. Folks stared and poked each other. Whispers whispered loud enough for a deaf man to hear was a constant occurrence and mean, nasty, untrue things were being said about her father. Miss Odessa had made Little Missy promise not to pay the wagging tongues no mind, but she was finding it almost impossible. She had never wanted to learn the art of fist fighting before, but now she did.

The preacher's words hung over her head like a dark cloud. They held back her desire to lash out at her father's foes and her conscience made her feel shameful, but she couldn't help but wonder why the other folks didn't seem to suffer from the same conviction. How come they could get away with being mean?

Preacher Shaddix slapped his hands together very loudly, as a means of making sure everybody was paying attention, and then he looked out over the congregation. "We are all neighbors here," he said, "and the scriptures tells us to love our neighbors."

His message rang out loud and clear and caused many people to shift uncomfortably in their seats. His message was indeed a powerful one but evidently it wasn't powerful enough to calm the troubled waters. The folks of Shadow Springs were divided and it appeared they were determined to stay that way.

Shaking the preacher's hand after the service turned into a ritual that most chose to forego. The Carter family and a few others shook his hand and thanked him for his spiritual guidance, but most everybody else walked past him as if he was invisible.

Mayor Digby and his wife stood on the sidewalk until Benton went to get the car and then they rushed over to where Kate Carter, her daughter and granddaughter were waiting. "This is unofficial, off the record but," the mayor said, catching Kate by the arm, "I thought you might want to have a talk with your son-in-law."

"And why would I want to do that?" Kate asked, quickly pushing his hand away.

"To talk some sense into him." The mayor's wife interrupted. "Surely Kate, you see that he should resign. His stubborn attitude is causing ill will. Folks are threatening to withdraw their money from the bank." She looked at Elizabeth Anne. "And look at the stress he's causing his sweet, little wife." She leaned close and shook her head. "She's as thin as a rail."

"Yes, she certainly is and don't you envy her for her high metabolism?" Kate smiled. "You've always had to struggle with your weight.

What a shame, Florence, you can't give her some of your unsightly fat."

"Ah." Mrs. Digby's mouth flew open. "How dare you insult me."

"And how dare you insult my son-in-law and my daughter," Kate huffed. "I don't…"

"Mother, please." Elizabeth Anne stepped forward. "Thank you, Mrs. Digby, for being concerned about my health." She moistened her lips and stood silently, as if she were gathering her thoughts.

Little Missy swallowed hard, and prayed her mother wouldn't break down in tears. She was making progress, becoming more like her old self, but she was still very fragile. Little Missy was worried this might cause her mother to have a setback.

"Mr. Mayor." Elizabeth Anne lowered her voice. "I'm glad this is unofficial because I unofficially want to tell you that my husband is a brilliant man. He is patient and forgiving, but he is also an advocate for justice and he will not relent until justice is done. He plans to pursue this investigation no matter where it takes him, even if it takes him to the mayor's office." Elizabeth Anne fixed her gaze and took a deep breath. "Do you have anything to hide, Mr. Mayor? If not, why aren't you helping my husband? Are you afraid of public opinion? Are you shirking your duty?" Her voice rose. "Are you?"

"Absolutely not," Mayor Digby answered. He puffed his chest and jutted his chin. "I'm insulted by your accusation."

"And I too, by yours, sir." Elizabeth Anne returned his indignation, refusing to be intimated. "As mayor, you should be working with Benton and the others." She pulled her dark glasses from her purse and casually put them on. "I'm sure we all have better things to do rather than stand in the hot sun, but if you choose to continue this conversation, may I suggest that we find a shade."

Mayor Digby shook his head and slowly exhaled. "No, that's not necessary." He cupped his hand under his wife's elbow and turned to leave. "Good day to you," he said over his shoulder.

"And good day to you," Elizabeth Anne replied. She stood stone-like, unmovable, until the couple crossed the parking lot and then she relaxed. "Thank goodness, they're gone," she said, trying to steady her hands. "I'm shaking like a leaf."

"Well, you would never have known," Kate Carter said grinning from ear to ear. "You reminded me of your father, take charge and to the point. Thomas would have been so proud of you."

"I'm kind of proud of myself, too. I haven't felt this strong in a long time." Elizabeth Anne hugged her mother. "I know Benton is upset and I want to be there for him."

"You have been. I've watched you these last few weeks. You've been strong and supportive." Kate put her hand over her heart. "You're becoming your father's daughter. I venture to say, it won't be long before you're running the mill. Thomas always hoped you would."

"I know." Elizabeth Anne dropped her head. "I'm not ready for that yet, but," she looked up, "maybe some day."

"I think I might want to run the mill when I grow up." Little Missy joined the conversation. "I've been thinking about asking Mr. Dewberry to give me a tour. Maybe even ask him to let me work for him when I get old enough. I might ask him to become my mentor."

"Oh, really?" Grandmother Kate looked surprised. "Now you're interested in touring the mill?" She looked at her daughter then turned back to Little Missy. "And now you're a Grady Dewberry fan?"

"Yes, and yes." She grinned.

"Oh, so you like Grady now? Is that what you're saying?"

"Yes, ma'am, I like Mr. Dewberry and his lady friend."

"Grady has a lady friend?" Kate Carter looked at Elizabeth Anne with a puzzled expression. Elizabeth Anne stared back and shrugged her shoulders.

"Tell us all about this lady friend of Grady's." Grandmother Kate said.

Chapter 16

James Everett banged on the front door and waited impatiently for Little Missy to let him in.

"Why are you here in the middle of the day?" she asked. "I thought you and Travis were going to Montgomery. I thought…"

"Shhh," James Everett covered her mouth and pulled her outside. "The sheriff picked up Travis and took him to the police station."

"Mmm mmm," Little Missy mumbled, pulling his hand away. "Travis has been arrested? Why?" She was taken aback. She couldn't imagine Travis going to jail. "I'll go get my father, he is home for lunch. He'll know what to do."

"No, stop, Travis hasn't been arrested. Sheriff Connelly and Mr. McIntyre, the detective from the FBI, wanted to talk to him, ask him some questions about daddy's death." James Everett spun her around. "Don't tell your daddy about Travis, just ask if you can go with me."

"Where are we going?"

"To Mr. Tucker's barn. I figure since he is in Texas this would be the best time to have a look around. We might get lucky."

"Father could drive us, the farm is several miles away."

"No, don't tell him where we're going. Where is your head, girl? Your daddy ain't gonna take part in searching Mr. Tucker's barn. Folks are already suspicious of him. If we were to find something they might accuse him of putting it there." He ran his hand through his hair. "Don't you know nothing?"

"I know…"

"I know, I know," James Everett stopped her. "I'm rude, you've told me that a million times."

Little Missy made a face. "Well, it's true. You are rude." She turned to go inside, but hesitated. "How are we going to get there?"

"I've got the truck, it's parked down the road, out of sight."

Little Missy's voice filled with uneasiness. "You're driving," she drew a calming breath and asked, "and where should I say we're going?"

"I don't know…make something up."

When she finally returned, James Everett looked at Little Missy as if she had suddenly grown two heads. "Are you crazy?" he asked, as he shoved two fishing poles and a can of worms into the back of his daddy's truck.

"Well, you said to make something up. How was I supposed to know Mr. Doddie was going to loan us his fishing poles and make me dig for worms?"

"You should have known you couldn't go fishing without…oh, for Pete's sake." James Everett threw up his hands. "Just get in."

"I'm not sure I want to. Travis said you know how to drive but…"

"Fine, you can walk." He opened the driver's door and climbed in. "I'm going with or without you," he said slamming the door. He adjusted the feather pillow behind his back, scooted up closer to the edge of the seat, and then he stretched his foot and mashed in the clutch. "You getting in or not?" he asked turning the key. The engine turned over and the truck rolled forward. James Everett stomped the break. "Well?"

"Okay, wait." Little Missy reluctantly got in. "Let's go, but please no speeding."

Speed was not the issue, bumps and deep ruts were. James Everett didn't take the main highway; instead he detoured onto the old original road and drove the back way to Mr. Tucker's farm. Little Missy remembered walking the road with her mother on her first visit to her grandmother's house. She marveled inwardly, at how much her life had changed since that day. She also marveled at how skillfully the young driver handled the truck, even though he had to stretch his legs in order to reach the pedals. The gears shifted without grinding, but the ride was rough.

Finally, James Everett pulled the truck off the road and under some low hanging limbs. "We're gonna have to walk the rest of the way." He shot Little Missy a warning look. "We need to keep our heads about us. Don't go getting scared on me now."

"Okay." She nodded, trying to conceal her nervousness. She scurried out of the truck and followed James Everett down the road and across the pasture. They climbed over the fence and ran, hunkering down, to the back of the barn.

"Daddy parked his truck over there." James Everett pointed to the back gate. "He left it running and then…" his voice quivered. "I found him." Sadness spread across his face, his eyes welled with tears. "Mama had waited until almost dark before she sent me to look for him. She said she figured he was drinking again and was passed out. She told me to try to sober him up before I brought him home, she didn't want the other kids to know.

Her eyes were full of hurt and disappointment, she had been so hopeful. It made me mad to see her like that." James Everett clinched his jaw. "It was dark, no light, except the moon. I couldn't see clearly, just the image of him leaning against the back wall. I called to him." James Everett's voice filled with anger. He turned his gaze toward Little Missy. "But he didn't move… so I walked over and kicked his leg. I shouted for him to get up and I called him a drunk. He still didn't move so I kicked him again, harder this time and I said, 'I hate you, I hate you, I wish you were dead.'" James Everett beat his fist into his hand and fought to keep the tears away. "I was so angry, so disgusted with him, but when I bent down and saw the blood and the gun…" His shoulders slumped. "I was upset with him. I said things I didn't mean…but I didn't hate him. I loved him. He was my daddy and I loved him," he sobbed. "I'm sorry, I'm so sorry I said those things."

Acting on impulse, Little Missy squeezed his arm. "I know, I know." A wrenching pain seized her heart. Her desire to take away his pain left her with a loss for words. She edged closer to him and waited, huddled up for a long time, not saying anything, just trying to comfort him by being close. She knew this was a hard thing for him to have to relive, to have to make peace with. She couldn't fathom the hurt he must be feeling.

James Everett tightened his throat, trying to control his emotions. His heart pounded so hard it ruffled his shirt. Blood rushed to his head, he felt dizzy. He wished he hadn't broke down, let his frustrations out. His pride told him he was weak, he had to pull himself together; he had to concentrate on why they were there. Finally, he pushed his anguish aside and cleared his throat. "Daddy didn't kill himself. I know he didn't."

Little Missy nodded.

The inside of the barn was dimly lit. Tiny streams of sunlight filtered down between the tall rafters and covered the hay bales with streaks of light. Dust particles floated downward, flitting about the ladder that was attached to the wall next to the tractor. Hay bales, stacked four bales high, blocked access to the overstuffed hayloft.

"I don't think Daddy hid anything up there," James Everett announced as he looked around. "We'll have to search down here." He headed toward an old tarp hanging down from an overhead beam. He carefully inched between a stack of boxes and some farm equipment. "Be careful not to move stuff," he said softly. "Don't want anybody to notice we've been here."

"Okay," Little Missy whispered. She moved toward the long row of feed barrels and fuel drums. As she searched, she wondered what she should be looking for. "Are we looking for money or some kind of record book?" she asked.

"I don't know," James Everett whispered back. "I've been thinking a lot about that. Daddy was a simple man, but he wasn't stupid. Whatever he hid he knew it was important." He wiggled through the maze of obstacles before finally making it to the tarp. He bent down and looked underneath. "Look," he shouted, forgetting to be quiet. "It's Mr. Tucker's truck." He grabbed the tarp and quickly jerked it back.

Little Missy ran over. "I thought he was in Texas. Why is he hiding his truck?"

James Everett's expression transformed from being confused to enlightened. "He's here, he's hiding out. Mr. Tucker ain't in Texas, he just wants everybody to think he is."

"But why?"

"Because he's got something to hide."

James Everett and Little Missy searched every inch of the truck. They looked in the glove compartment, under the seat and inside the ashtray. They pulled down the sun visors, but found nothing.

James Everett stood on the running board and did a brief scan of the bed. "Nothing except the fact that he's hiding his truck," he said, walking around to Little Missy. "He's probably holed up in the house and I bet…" he stopped mid sentence and put his hand up to his ear. "I hear a car," he said. "Quick, hide!" James Everett snatched the tarp closed and motioned for Little Missy to be quiet. They squatted next to the truck and listened as the car drove through the gate and inside the barn. Two doors opened and closed and two sets of fast walking footsteps stormed toward where they were. Angry voices belonging to Darby Brooks and Hershel Tucker bickered back and forth.

"I'm sick and tired of being cooped up in your apartment. What did Neville say?" Hershel asked.

"I've already told you." Darby answered. "Mr. Boggs didn't say anything. He and two inspectors from the FBI went straight back to Mr. Langford's office and waited until he returned from lunch and then they sent Ivy out and told her to shut the door and not let anybody in."

"What did they talk about, could you hear?"

"No, not with Ivy Holcomb standing guard. She stood there like a hawk and she wouldn't answer questions. She told me to go back to work." Darby slung her hair away from her face. "You should have fired her years ago. I told you she was trouble."

"Yeah, you told me a lot of things, Darby, that's why we're in this mess." Hershel shoved his hands into his pockets. "I should never have listened to you and your wild get rich quick scheme. I should have made you put the money back. I shouldn't have gotten involved."

"Now, you wait a minute, Hershel Tucker, don't you dare start blaming me for all this. You were more than willing to participate." She wiggled her body. "As a matter of fact, you seemed to enjoy what I offered…I certainly didn't hear you complain."

"No, I didn't mean that…I just wish things hadn't turned out the way they have." Hershel paced back and forth, a few steps toward the tarp and a few steps back. His actions made the children nervous. If he moved the tarp they would surely be discovered.

"If Wiley hadn't caught us," Hershel said. "If he hadn't found the books, if he hadn't figured out what you were…uh…we were up to, then maybe we could have put the money back."

"Well, it's too late for what-ifs." Darby pulled a lace handkerchief from her purse and blotted her face. "And it's too late to give the money back. It's only a matter of time before Mr. Boggs and the inspectors trace everything back to us…" she paused and started looking around, "unless we can find those books. If Wiley hadn't taken them we'd be in the clear and Ivy Holcomb would be sitting in jail." Darby used her handkerchief as a fan.

"You have to admit, Hershel, it was brilliant of me to make it look as if your secretary was the embezzler." She chuckled softly. "It would give me great pleasure to see the old battle axe in jail."

"Yes, Darby, it was brilliant, but none of that matters now. We've got to find those books, they've got to be here someplace." Hershel stopped pacing. "We've searched the loft and out back, where haven't we looked?"

"We've searched every inch of this stupid barn. Why do you keep insisting Wiley hid them here?"

"Because of something he said." Hershel's brow wrinkled. "He said, 'they're under your nose, ask your girlfriend.'"

"And what did he mean by that?"

"How am I supposed to know? You're the brilliant one." Hershel answered sarcastically. "What did he mean? What were you offering him?"

"Are you jealous, Hershel?" Darby shot him a menacing look.

"Not jealous, just realistic. I know how persuasive you can be."

Darby rushed over. "What are you accusing me of…being unfaithful?" She smirked. "You're the one carrying a torch for Kate Carter. You think I haven't noticed? You should have known she was never going to return your affections. Her husband's death didn't change a thing." Darby shook her finger in Hershel's face. "You're a stupid old fool, Hershel Tucker." She laughed a haughty laugh.

"You're old enough to be my father. What did I ever see in you?" Hershel's hand came down hard across her face. He grabbed her by the shoulders and shook her violently. "Watch your mouth or I..."

"You'll what?" Darby taunted. Blood trickled out the corner of her mouth. "You'll kill me, too." She snatched loose from Hershel and stared at him. "I started the embezzlement and I falsified the books, but at least I didn't kill Mr. Holloway."

Darby's crushing words caused James Everett to falter. His strength vanished. He went limp. Little Missy grabbed his arm in an effort to stable him, but she could tell he was seething, struggling to hold back his anger. Miss Brooks' admission finally confirmed what he had known all along. His daddy had not committed suicide. Wiley Holloway had been vindicated. His last actions were admirable, his family could be proud of him.

"I didn't mean to kill him." Hershel gritted his teeth. "I tried to talk some sense into him, I offered him money, but he wouldn't listen. I only meant to scare him with the gun, but he got all high and mighty on me. He started preaching right and wrong and demanding we go to the sheriff...I couldn't do that. I tried to explain that I had too much to lose, but he kept on and on...I lost my temper." Hershel Tucker's eyes darkened with evil. "He was nothing but a low down drunk, he had no right to judge me."

Little Missy felt the muscles in James Everett's arm tighten. His breathing became labored. His jaw clinched tight with rage. It was obvious he was not prepared to deal with the animosity that had built up inside him. "No," he shouted, springing up before Little Missy could stop him. He ripped back the tarp, catching Mr. Tucker and Darby Brooks by surprise. "You killed my daddy!" James Everett lunged forward with the velocity of a raging bull. He plowed into his daddy's murderer with such force that he lifted him off his feet and slammed him to the ground. "You killed him, you killed him!" He repeated, punching wildly.

Darby jumped back and screamed. She dropped her handkerchief and started flailing the young boy with her pocketbook. James Everett ignored her blows. His overpowering desire for revenge strengthened his assault to the point of rendering his victim breathless and struggling to fend off his assailant.

Little Missy tried disarming Miss Brooks by grabbing her handbag. "Stop, stop," she yelled, tugging the bottom half of the purse. "We know the truth and we're going to tell."

Darby was stunned by her threat. She suddenly stopped and turned loose of the purse straps, ending the tug of war. She held her hands up as a sign of surrender and stepped back. Her dark eyes widened, she realized their scheme was about to be exposed and they were trapped. She looked at Little Missy, holding her gaze, searching for a chink in her armor. "Who are you going to tell?" she asked.

"My father and the sheriff." Little Missy yelled, raising her voice enough to get James Everett's attention. He looked up. "Come on," she told him. Her voice was shaky, filled with fear.

James Everett fought his impulse to give one last punch. He realized his actions had put he and Little Missy in a lot of danger. He relaxed his fist, stood up and walked over to where she was standing.

Mr. Tucker gasped and rolled over. "Okay, kids," he sputtered. "We give up." He slowly pulled himself to his feet, staggered forward and braced against Darby's car. "Let me catch my breath and then we'll talk," he said, breathing deeply. "It seems you have the upper hand." He shifted his eyes toward Darby and gave her a slight nod, motioning for her to circle around the kids. She twitched her head, signaling that she understood. "What y'all heard ain't exactly the truth." Hershel grinned, waiting for Darby to get into position. "We need to discuss this."

From the corner of her eye, Little Missy watched Darby's movement. She tried to conceal her intentions by pretending she was going to pick up her handkerchief but in a split second she rushed forward with her arms spread wide. Mr. Tucker followed suit by lunging forward, trying to corral the children but Little Missy took a wild swing with the pocketbook. She hit Hershel Tucker hard across the side of his face, knocking him into Darby. They both toppled to the ground. "Run," she yelled, "Run."

James Everett grabbed the handkerchief and led the way out of the barn and across the pasture. They didn't look back until they were inside the truck and headed down the main highway. The old road was too bumpy to make a fast getaway.

James Everett asked. "Do you see them? Are they following us?"

"Yes, I see Miss Brooks' car pulling out into the road. Hurry, James Everett, hurry." Little Missy's hands were shaking. "What will they do to us? Do you think Mr. Tucker will kill us, too?"

James Everett stretched his leg and pressed down on the gas pedal. "They'll have to run us down, if they do?" He glanced in the rearview mirror. Darby's powder blue Bel Air was about a half mile away but was fast approaching, hugging the curves and floating over the dips in the road. "She's gaining on us," he muttered under his breath, as she got closer. "Is Mr. Tucker in there with her?"

Little Missy rolled down her window. "I don't see him," she said staring in the side mirror, "but he could be hiding in the backseat."

"Yeah, you might be right," James Everett said, pressing the pedal all the way to the floor. After a brief hesitation, the old truck gradually started to get faster and faster but it was no match for the car. Darby was about to overtake them. She started honking her horn and waving for them to pull over, but James Everett refused. He kept the pedal down and eased the truck over the centerline. "Can't let her get around, she could block us." He turned his attention back to the road. A sharp curve and a bridge would be coming up soon; he was going to have to slow down. Darby would have to slow down too, but if she didn't…if she didn't. "This is getting dangerous," he said taking his foot off the gas. "Access to the old road is just past the curve, hold on," he ordered. "We're gonna make a short detour."

Little Missy braced against the dashboard and prepared for the hard bump. Her face was ghostly white and her adrenalin was running high.

James Everett hugged the curve and then made a sharp turn onto the narrow, dirt and gravel, one-lane road. It veered off to the right, behind a long row of overgrown plum bushes and continued on to an old wooden bridge. James Everett slowed down to a crawl and steered the wheels so they would line up with the wide wooden planks. The loud rumble of the boards bumping up and down, as the tires rolled over them filled the cab and brought Little Missy to the realization that she had been so immersed in her emotions she hadn't realized she had twisted her shirttail into a knot. Her hair was a mess from flying in the wind, but she didn't care. She was anxious for the chase to end.

As soon as they crossed the bridge, James Everett stopped and leaned out his window. "I don't see her, she must have gone straight." He sighed. "I think we lost her."

The tremor in his voice kept Little Missy silent. She waited a long time without saying a word, but finally his gaze met hers. "What now?" she asked.

They held their breath, listened and patiently waited for several minutes. Once James Everett was convinced it was safe, he started the truck and followed the road back to the main highway. The nagging question of what to do next had been evaded long enough. Little Missy was determined to push for an answer but suddenly she looked up and saw Sheriff Connelly's car coming toward them. "This has to be divine intervention," she said with excitement. "He's probably bringing Travis home. Pull over, make him stop."

James Everett carefully inched the truck off the shoulder of the road. He leaped out and flagged the sheriff down. Travis sat in the backseat, looking shocked and surprise.

"What's going on?" the sheriff asked.

"It wasn't suicide," James Everett shouted, unable to remain calm. "Daddy was murdered and Mr. Tucker did it."

Travis leaned across the seat. "How do you know? What have you been up to?"

"Me and Little Missy were in his barn, we heard him. He and Miss Brooks are stealing money from the bank."

"Stealing, are you sure?" Sheriff Connelly interrupted.

"Yeah, I'm sure," he answered, "and you've got to arrest them."

Chapter 17

The sheriff didn't arrest anybody, he didn't chase after Darby Brooks or search for Hershel Tucker. He calmly told James Everett he was too young to be driving. "I've turned a blind eye before but I better not catch you doing it again." He held out his hand. "I admire your ability, son, but the law is the law. Do you understand?"

James Everett lowered his head and slowly handed him the truck keys. "Yes, sir," he mumbled softly. He shot Little Missy a sideward glance, hoping she wouldn't see his red face.

Sheriff Connelly pitched the keys to Travis and told him to drive home and wait for him there. He had more questions for them but first he was going to take Little Missy back to her grandmother's house.

Little Missy swallowed hard. His words sent a wave of nausea over her. She didn't relish the thought of riding home in the back of a police car. Her fishing story would to be revealed as a hoax and punishment would surely follow. She felt confident Sheriff Connelly would lecture her about the trespassing crime she and James Everett had committed. Her father would certainly remind her of the evils of deception, her mother was bound to cry and Grandmother Kate would probably be overcome with shame. Being perceived as the black sheep of the family was horrifying. Her dread caused her much pain, but the agony she suffered when the sheriff parked in the driveway was indescribable.

Mrs. Carter and Elizabeth Anne almost fainted when Sheriff Connelly let Little Missy out of the backseat. Miss Odessa threw up her hands in shock and shouted, "What has this world come to that the sheriff would arrest a poor, helpless child." She wrung her hands and spun around in circles. "Dodie, Dodie," she called, begging him to come to the rescue.

He immediately took charge, sat them all down at the kitchen table and told them, "Let the lawman have his say."

The sheriff explained the situation and then he told Little Missy to recount her story, tell word for word what had been said and done. He listened intently but made no comment, other than to say that the FBI was investigating and they needed proof, a lot of proof, before they would make an arrest. He told Little Missy she would be questioned again, but in the mean time; he expected her and James Everett to stop their snooping and to stay out of harm's way.

After the sheriff left the Carter's house he went by Mr. Tucker's farm, found him at home and questioned him about the bank discrepancies. Hershel told him that he had just gotten back from Texas and knew nothing about what was going on at the bank other than what Darby Brooks had told him on the phone. He said he intended to go into work the next morning and see if he could figure things out. "I'm sure I will be able to clear everything up, I just need to get a good night's sleep first," he told the sheriff.

"I doubt this is going to be cleared up in one day, Hershel. Neville Boggs and the FBI have been combing through the bank records for more than a week now, and they are highly disturbed. It doesn't look good." Sheriff Connelly walked to his car, opened the door and stepped one foot inside. "Neville came to me several months ago when he was finishing his audit…there was trouble even back then."

"Oh, really, why didn't you tell me, why wasn't I notified?"

"Because some things take time." The sheriff removed his hat. "Is there anything you want to tell me?" he asked.

"Of course not, I'm completely in the dark, but I'm sure we'll be able to clear this up." Hershel's answer seemed rehearsed. "I'm not worried."

"I wish I could say the same." Sheriff Connelly sat down and closed the door. "I wish I could say the same," he repeated before driving away.

The light from the wall sconces had grown dim and the evening shadows had disappeared when the sheriff drove away from the Holloway house. James Everett felt as if he was beating his head against a brick wall. "Why won't he listen to me?" he asked Travis. "I don't think he believes me."

"No, it's not that," Travis told him. "The sheriff and I talked for a long time at the station. He told me he's had doubts about daddy's suicide and Hershel Tucker all along."

"Then, why ain't he done something about it?"

"He needs proof."

"I showed him the handkerchief, I told him what me and Little Missy heard, how much more proof does he need?"

"Well," Travis said, "It sure would help if we had those books."

"Where do you think Daddy hid them? We've looked everywhere."

"I don't know, but we can't solve the mystery tonight." Travis looked at his watch. "It's late, let's get some sleep, so we'll have a clear head tomorrow."

Sleep did not come easy for James Everett. He felt dejected and downcast, as if he were the only one with a blazing desire to seek justice for his daddy. He thought about talking to his mother, but the sheriff's visit had upset her so much he just couldn't bring himself to burden her anymore. He was anxious to tell her that her husband's last actions were honorable, but he decided it probably would be best to wait. The sheriff had reiterated several times that he should keep quiet until the case was officially over. James Everett understood the logic, he didn't want to compromise the investigation, but patience did not come easy for him. That was one of the reasons he didn't want to go along with Travis's early morning suggestion to take Little Missy fishing. He knew his brother was trying to keep them busy, out of trouble, and his intentions were well meaning, but he definitely was not in the mood to take Little Missy fishing. She had never fished before; he knew it was going to be a disaster.

Little Missy's parent's stern tongue lashing the night before had her convinced she would never be allowed to leave the house again. She was amazed that Travis had been able to persuade them to reverse their decision.

"Make sure you get the hook wet." James Everett sat on the bank behind her. He was unhappy about having to be there and he was determined to show it. "You can't expect to catch anything if you don't put the hook in the water."

"I'm trying, really I am, but the limbs keep getting in the way." Her hands shook as she jerked her tangled fishing line out of the trees. "I think I'm done for the day. I don't want to kill another worm just so I can sling it off or lose it in a tangle of tree limbs? Who's idea was it for us to go fishing today, anyway?"

"It was my idea." Travis spoke up. "Since y'all had all the fishing gear in the truck and because Sheriff Connelly told me not to let y'all out of my sight, I figured we might as well have a little fun." He swapped fishing poles with Little Missy. "Hold mine and I'll bait yours and throw it out for you."

"Thank you," she said, "I appreciate your patience; James Everett isn't as kind. He expects me to know everything, without being taught."

Travis chuckled. "That's my little brother, for sure." He looked around, "Why are you being such a spoilsport?"

"Cause I think we should be looking for those books," his voice was sharp, "or at least trying to figure out the clue Daddy left behind." He stood up and held out Darby's handkerchief. It lay flat, fully unfolded, in his hand. "It's a match," he said, looking up. "The same cloth and the same lace pattern." He walked over to Little Missy and Travis. "Here, let me show you." He pulled the other handkerchief out of his back pocket and gingerly slid it from its plastic wrap. "See, it looks the same and smells the same." He held it out.

Little Missy leaned close and sniffed. "A Joyful Rose." She smiled.

"Yeah," James Everett agreed. "We know Darby Brooks wears that perfume and we definitely know both handkerchiefs belong to her and…"

"Where did you get that?" Travis asked.

"From Miss Ella, Daddy gave it to her. He told her he had discovered some wrongdoing and he wanted her to hold on to it. We think it's a clue."

"Here, let me see," Travis laid down the fishing pole. "How long have you had this handkerchief?"

"Months," James Everett answered, spreading it out for the first time, so that it would lay flat over the other one. As the last fold unfolded a little brown piece of paper fell to the ground.

Travis picked it up. " It's daddy's handwriting…it says…. Don't tell Mary Ruth."

"It's a clue," Little Missy squealed. "But who's Mary Ruth? Isn't she your mother?"

"Yeah, but what does it mean? Don't tell Mama what?" James Everett looked at Travis. His brother looked as if someone had just splashed him in the face with a glass of cold water.

"I know what it means. I know where Daddy hid the books." Travis' eyes sparkled with excitement. "Get the stuff and follow me," he yelled running up the bank to the truck. He yanked opened the passenger's door and pulled back the floor mat.

"What are you doing?" James Everett piled the fishing poles in the bed and stood on the running board, peering over his brother's shoulder. Little Missy couldn't see so she ran to the other side and slid across the seat. Travis reached over, ran his hands along the bottom of the dashboard and removed a piece of hard cardboard. He then stretched his arm and felt deeper and deeper into a hollowed out space behind the glove compartment. "This is where Daddy hid his liquor from Mama. I found it one time and he made me promise not to tell Mary Ruth." He pulled out the books and flipped through the pages. "They have been here all along."

"What are we waiting for?" James Everett asked. "Let's take them to the sheriff's office. You said he needed proof…we'll give him proof."

"No," Little Missy suggested eagerly. "We need to take them to the bank, give them to Mr. Boggs. He can call the sheriff."

Travis looked uncomfortably at James Everett and asked, "Are you ready for this?" His tone, filled with concern for his younger brother, reminded Little Missy of the turmoil her friend must be feeling. She took a hard look at James Everett. His expression was guarded. All the color had drained from his face.

"Are you ready?" Travis asked, challenging him for an answer. "Amid all that's happened, I just want to make sure you're okay."

"This ain't about me. This is about Daddy…I want to set the record straight," James Everett said with restraint. "I'm ready, let's go."

A battle raged within Little Missy's mind as they drove to the bank. This was the opportunity she and James Everett had been waiting for, the chance to expose how Mr. Tucker had sabotaged her father's and Wiley Holloway's reputation. Both men had been unjustly accused. She was desperate to deliver the proof, desperate to bring peace to those who were under the threat of foreclosure and she was desperate to savor the feeling of accomplishment. For months she had anticipated this moment, but her nerves were beginning to get the better of her.

Once they arrived at the bank, she wasted no time in leading the way up the steps and into the main lobby. Her intentions were to request a private meeting with her father so that Travis and James Everett could hand over the books, but to her surprise, she found Ivy Holcomb standing guard in front of her father's office.

"I'm sorry, sweetie," said Mrs. Holcomb. "Your father can't be disturbed."

"Yes, ma'am, but this is an emergency. I really need to see him." She glanced backward. Travis held the books tightly under his arm. "We have something to give him."

"What about Mr. Boggs?" James Everett asked, stepping forward. "Can we see him?"

"He's in the conference room with Mr. Langford." Mrs. Holcomb leaned over and whispered, "Mr. McIntyre and two more agents are in there. They're all waiting for the sheriff."

"That's great," Little Missy said, hoping to persuade Ivy Holcomb to change her mind. "Sheriff Connelly will want to see what we have, too. It really is important. May we…"

Travis nudged Little Missy, causing her to turn around. Her heart leaped with surprise. The sheriff and Hershel Tucker were entering the bank.

"I'm sorry, but you're going to have to wait. You can't see your father now." Mrs. Holcomb disappeared but returned within seconds and shooed Little Missy and her friends away. "Come back later," she ordered.

They backed away but did not leave. They stood against the wall and watched as Benton Langford and the other gentlemen filed out of the conference room. Their demeanor was that of discovery, an uncovering of a crime, a sense of confrontation. Mr. McIntyre motioned to his agents. "Bring the woman out here," he ordered.

Darby Brooks looked frightened, almost to the point of panic, as they led her from the room where she had been sequestered. Her reaction to seeing Hershel Tucker was steeped with relief and despair. She made a feeble attempt to portray an air of confidence, but it was apparent she was riddled with fear.

Hershel avoided looking in her direction. He gave her profile a quick glance but then he turned his attention to Benton and the men standing next to him. "Gentlemen, I believe you have discovered a problem." His voice was calm and mater-of-fact. "Sheriff Connelly has briefed me on the situation and after a sleepless night, I think I have come up with a solution." He extended his hand to Mr. McIntyre. "I see Neville has brought out the big guns." Mr. Tucker sneered sarcastically. "The FBI, I'm impressed." He shook his hand firmly and then said, "I see no reason to prolong this." He stepped forward and opened his office door. "Allow me a brief moment to retrieve something from my desk and I'll meet you in the conference room."

The sheriff looked at Mr. McIntyre for confirmation. He nodded.

Ivy Holcomb reached out, touched her boss's arm, and whispered softly, "I'll be glad to get it for you, Hershel, what do you need?"

He waved his hand. "Don't bother, Ivy, you've been the perfect employee and have served me well all these years, but ..." his voice was tender, "I have to do this myself."

She locked her eyes on his face. He looked destroyed, anguished, broken. Hershel Tucker looked guilty. Ivy felt a sudden wave of sorrow. Her stomach churned, her heart sank with the fear that something horrible was about to happen. "Please let me help you," she pleaded.

"No." Hershel stared at her as if he were in deep thought. His shoulders slumped, his chin trembled and he let out a sigh. He almost spoke, but instead, he turned his gaze toward Darby Brooks and smiled an empty smile. Then he entered his office and closed the door.

Everyone stood, unmoving as though they were paralyzed. The atmosphere became thick with tension. Silent stillness wafted over them. Time stood still for a brief moment, but then Little Missy realized she should use this opportunity to present the books. She took them from Travis and swiftly walked to her father. She held them out. "We found these and we think," she gestured for the two brothers to join her, "this is the proof you've been needing."

Benton was surprised to see his daughter; he gave her a puzzled look. "What?"

"A set of altered books," Travis explained. "They seem to indicate…"

Darby broke loose from her guards and lunged forward. "Where did you get those?" she demanded, glaring at Little Missy. "You little brat." She attempted to grab the evidence, but the agents quickly restrained her. She squirmed and resisted, but to no avail. They cuffed her hands together and held her by the arms.

Neville Boggs took the books and quickly examined them. "Just as I suspected. These positively prove an intentional alteration of financial records." He looked directly at Little Missy for the first time since the bathroom incident. "Good job, young lady. You and your friends are to be commended."

"Yes, but," James Everett proclaimed fiercely. "They also prove my daddy didn't…"

His argument was shockingly interrupted by a loud bang. The sound of a gunshot rang out from inside Mr. Tucker's office. Instantly, the sheriff pulled his gun and rushed forward, only to discover that the door was locked.

Mr. McIntyre pushed him aside. "Stand back," he commanded, giving the door a hard, quick kick. It flung open and he and Sheriff Connelly rushed over and slowly opened Hershel's private office door. He was slumped back in his expensive leather chair behind his mahogany desk, surrounded by all the things he held dear, his trophies and awards. His eyes were open and his arms hung limply at his side. A long trail of blood flowed from his temple and ran down the side of his face. Tightly gripped in his hand, was his pistol, the very one he had used to kill Wiley Holloway.

Ivy Holcomb and Benton Langford rushed in, but stopped abruptly at the doorway. Ivy gasped at the scene and let out a terrifying scream. "He's dead, he's dead," she cried.

Benton put his arm around her and led her back out into the hallway. "I'm sorry, Mrs. Holcomb," he said, trying to comfort her. He looked at Sheriff Connelly, hoping for instructions on what to do. He had not anticipated such a tragic outcome and he was unsure how to proceed.

The sheriff immediately told the agents to escort everyone into the conference room, but Darby became inconsolable. She let out a sharp groan and slumped to the floor. "No, no," she lamented. "Why, Hershel, why? I told you we should run. Why didn't you listen?"

Repulsed by Darby's mournful display, Ivy stared down at her with disgust. She would offer her no sympathy; her sorrows were of her own making. She had participated in the evil plot from the very beginning and it was only right that she suffer the consequences. "I ask you the same thing. Why, why were you so greedy?" she asked.

Darby sadly turned away in shame, but Ivy bent down, grabbed her jaw and forced her to look at her. "You caused so much pain for so many. Why?"

Darby jerked away, refusing to answer.

Neville placed his hand on the small of Ivy's back. "Mrs. Holcomb, please," he said, encouraging her to follow him and the others. "People are watching," he whispered.

Frantic bank customers and employees were pushing and shoving, trying to see what was going on. "The bank is closed, please go home," Benton spoke up, blocking their view with his body. He turned to his daughter. "You too, Katherine, Sheriff Connelly can talk to you and your friends later. You don't need to be here in the center of all this chaos."

"Yes, sir," she answered, suppressing her curiosity. As much as she wanted to stay, she knew her father was right. She waved to him and slowly moved down the hall to where Travis was standing. "Where's James Everett?" she asked.

"I don't know, I thought he was with you."

"No, I thought he…" Little Missy stopped; her hands went instinctively to her mouth. "I know where he is," she whispered and then swiftly turned the corner and slipped back to Mr. Tucker's office. The door was open; she could see James Everett standing next to the body, trance-like, frozen and unmoving. His expression was blank. His eyes were empty and his voice was harsh and loud. "You coward, you coward," he shouted.

Chapter 18

The news of Hershel Tucker's death spread throughout the entire community, as if it were a tornado. Within three hours of Darby Brooks being led away in handcuffs, a crowd had gathered around the front steps of the bank and was loudly demanding answers from Sheriff Connelly, Benton Langford and Neville Boggs.

"Withdrawing your money and placing blame isn't going to bring about justice," the sheriff yelled. "These men are working with the authorities, but it's going to take time." He exchanged troubled looks with the men standing next to him.

Benton stepped forward. "I assure you, your money is safe and no one is going to be foreclosed on at this time. We're working to accurately account for all missing funds and expect to have a resolution very soon. Please," he raised his hands to quiet the shouts, "please go home."

The angry chant rose from the crowd again. "We want our money, we want our money." Their apparent agitated mood caused the sheriff to swiftly move to the edge of the porch. "Settle down, settle down," he demanded with much authority. "Mr. Langford asked y'all to go home and now I'm telling you to." He raised his voice. "I won't put up with this lynch mob behavior."

The protesters reacted by mumbling and complaining but did not make an effort to disperse or to be quiet until Neville Boggs reluctantly stepped forward. A sudden hush fell hard and heavy, like a wet woolen blanket, as he cleared his throat and nervously shifted his weight from his right foot to his left. His face was whiter than cotton and he was sweating profusely. It was obvious he felt ill at ease. "This embezzlement was slowly and fraudulently implemented and the crime carries penalties punishable by imprisonment and restitution." He wiped the sweat from his forehead, quickly stepped back and nodded to the crowd, signaling that he was finished; he had nothing more to say.

The audience was stunned by the fact that he had spoken more than three words in one sentence and they were confused. He sounded as if he had quoted from a dictionary. What did he say? What did he mean?

After a long period of discreet whispers and multiple attempts by the crowd members to decipher the meaning of Neville's short, choppy statement, the sheriff finally spoke up. "Hershel Tucker and Darby Brooks were greedy. They betrayed us all," he said, shaking his head. "Unfortunately, there is no means of justice for Hershel, but I intend to do everything within my power to see that Miss Brooks is punished to the full extent of the law."

Loud whispers and stinging comments rumbled throughout the crowd, but eventually tempers calmed and everyone dispersed peacefully. The next few days, however, were tumultuous, like a powder keg, ready to ignite any minute. Mr. McIntyre and his agents worked closely with the sheriff's department to keep the angry accusations and name calling at bay. They realized that if the situation continued to fester with distrust and backbiting Mr. Tucker's funeral could become volatile very quickly, so they stood ready and alert.

The parking lot of the funeral home was packed. Vehicles filled every space and lined both sides of the street. Local dignitaries and common folks alike scurried across the hot pavement and lined up on the sidewalk. The slow-moving line outside was made tolerable by the misconception that the inside would be a cooler place to wait, but once inside the reality was disappointing. Everybody was sandwiched together within the confines of the receiving area and was instantly overpowered by unpleasant smells of body odor, wilting flowers and a mixture of perfumes and aftershave. Lack of space coupled with everyone's astonishment over the newly revealed evidence hampered the movement of the viewing line. Everyone seemed intent on debating, denying and disputing the fact that Hershel was capable of committing such a heinous act and were adamant about blaming Darby and ridiculing Wiley Holloway for getting involved.

Since Mr. Tucker had no immediate family, there was no one to receive condolences at the head of the casket, so Sheriff Connelly stood guard and encouraged everyone to keep moving.

Ivy Holcomb and the members of the Board of Directors were allowed the privilege of a private viewing but Benton Langford refused. He felt duty bound to show respect to the former bank president, in spite of the crime he had committed. But Benton didn't want to be accused of receiving special treatment, so he and his family stood in line like all the rest.

The enormous number of mourners included people mourning the loss of the image Hershel Tucker had portrayed, a dear friend and neighbor. Some people were there out of obligation and some were there out of curiosity, but James Everett and his family were there because they needed closure. Mary Ruth Holloway and all six of her children showed no remorse as they stared down into the casket. "This man," she whispered so only her children could hear, "will face judgment far worse than anything we could ever impose. His deeds have shown his true character."

"But it ain't right, Mama," James Everett spoke purposely loud; he wanted the people to hear him. "He's a murderer and a thief and nobody wants to admit it. They all act like his death is a great loss."

"It is a great loss, son." She kept her voice low. "Because his actions sealed his fate."

"His actions sealed Daddy's fate too, don't you see?" He spun around and angrily marched off. Mrs. Holloway tried to grab him, but he slipped through the crowd. She told Travis to find him, so he stretched his neck, hoping to see which way he went, but the crowd was too thick. Finally he saw Little Missy and her family, so he weaved his way over. "Have you seen James Everett? He's upset."

"No," Kate Carter answered, standing on her tiptoes. "He must have gone that way." She pointed to the side door. "There is no way he could get through here without us seeing him."

Travis nodded and wormed his way back toward the exit.

"May I help look for him?" Little Missy asked, already stepping out of line.

"Elizabeth Anne looked at her husband. "I think she should, he certainly needs a friend."

Benton agreed so Little Missy slowly inched her way into the small hallway. Her intentions were to go out the front door and circle around to the side entrance but she suddenly heard James Everett loudly whisper her name. He stepped out from around the corner and motioned for her to join him. "The mayor and Judge Wilkes are in there." He placed his finger to his lips. "They're in there conniving."

"In where?" she asked.

"There," he pointed to the funeral director's office. "Come on."

Light spilling out from underneath the office door and the sound of muffled voices caused Little Missy to feel a sudden sense of shame. Eavesdropping was wrong. "I'm not sure we should…"

James Everett met her protest with a stern look. "Shhh," he ordered. "Listen." He pressed his ear to the door and motioned for her to do the same.

Her sympathy for her friend overrode her misgivings, so she complied. She tried to control her breathing, so she could concentrate on the words spoken from the other side of the door.

"I've come to the conclusion that we must downplay this fiasco," said Judge Wilkes. "Hershel made us look like fools. We trusted him…I can't believe he would let that little bimbo lead him astray."

"I agree. We've got to stop this catastrophe before folks lose all confidence." The mayor cleared his throat. "Like I said before, I think we should portray Darby as the mastermind, present the scenario of an older man being seduced by a much younger woman."

"Yeah, okay, but what are we going to do about Wiley Holloway's murder?" asked the judge. "That can't be explained away as lust and we can't just sweep that under the carpet. We're going to have to deal with it. Accessory charges will probably be filed against Darby."

James Everett pressed his ear harder against the door.

The mayor's voice sounded angry. "We're between a rock and a hard place. The embezzlement and Hershel's suicide is bad enough without having to deal with a sorry, lowdown drunk who decided he wanted to be the voice of justice. If he had gone to the sheriff first, instead of trying to be a hero, he wouldn't have gotten himself killed and we wouldn't be in this predicament."

James Everett staggered back, away from the door. He looked heartbroken. "Sorry, lowdown drunk," he softly repeated the mayor's words. "I...I can't...I." He cast his eyes downward and stared at the floor.

"Don't listen to them, they're despicable human beings." Little Missy reached out to her friend, but he snatched away and started pounding on the door.

"Sorry, lowdown drunk!" he shouted over and over. He tightened his fists and pounded harder and harder until Judge Wilkes and the mayor opened the door. "Wiley Holloway was my daddy," he said lowering his arms. "That sorry, lowdown drunk was my daddy!"

The judge and the mayor stood speechless, staring down at the children with no expression whatsoever, as if they were staring at a blank wall.

James Everett moved back with distain. He clenched his teeth, narrowed his brow and said, "My daddy was more of a man than y'all will ever be." Then he spat at their feet and stormed off without telling anyone where he was going or when he would be back.

Chapter 19

"Everybody is entitled to dey opinion, but if you ask me, we're better off without the likes of dem two." Miss Odessa pulled out a chair and sat down at the kitchen table. "Hershel Tucker walked around town, pretending he was an upstanding, law abiding, good Christian man, when all the time, he was sneaking around with dat little Jezebel." She poured two cups of coffee and waited for Dodie to sit down. "I had her figured out a long time ago. Her prissy hips and revealing clothes was a dead giveaway. I didn't need no magnifying glass to see dat she was a conniving cheat."

"Yep, I agree with you bout dat Darby Brooks, but Mr. Hershel was a great disappointment to me. I never figured he'd become a crook." Dodie tilted his cup so the coffee would run into his saucer. "I hardly think it's fair the way folks are carrying on about his death being such a tragedy." He raised his saucer, blew away the steam and slurped loudly. "Seems to me dat his sins should be called out and dealt with. Death is final and the Lord will judge him, but dat don't give folks the right to make him out to be something he wasn't."

"The fact is, he was human," said Miss Odessa. "He made some bad choices and he should have been held accountable, but instead, everybody is lamenting over him and acting like he was a saint."

"Who was a saint?" Kate Carter asked, making her way into the kitchen.

"Hershel Tucker." Miss Odessa poured another cup of coffee and handed it to her. "Me and Dodie was commenting on how folks are making such a fuss over him. The sheriff stopped by last night. He said he's calling in deputies from the next county cause he's afraid the funeral is gonna turn into a spectacle. He said he's expecting more people than the church can hold."

"I don't doubt that. The funeral home was so packed you could hardly turn around." Kate took the coffee and leaned against the sink. "And some folks were acting mean and devilish, more concerned about Hershel's reputation than the crime he committed. They made snide remarks about Benton and badmouthed Wiley, refused to see that he put his life on the line trying to bring about justice, and they were ready to send Darby off to jail for the rest of her life." Kate shook her head. "I agree that Darby should go to jail but they act like it was all her fault. Hershel could have stopped her if he'd wanted to. He chose to do what he did."

"Dats right, Darby Brooks and Hershel Tucker were nothing but thieves." Dodie stood up. "But nobody sees dat, dey wants to blame Mr. Benton for not uncovering their evil plot sooner, but dey ain't taking into account that Neville Boggs was bamboozled by dem, too."

Kate raised her cup and said, "You can blame Hershel for that; he started rumors before Benton ever got here. He had already announced his retirement; he and Darby were going to run away with all that money, but he hadn't counted on Wiley finding those books. Hershel needed to swap them but once that became impossible, his only hope was to destroy Benton's creditability. He knew it wouldn't take him long to discover the embezzlement."

"And Mr. Benton was too much of a gentleman to confront him bout his name calling." Dodie picked up his hat and walked to the door. "I seen his face when he thought nobody was looking. It saddened him to know that folks were judging him unkindly, but I reckon he loved his family too much to burden dem with his disappointments. Men do thangs like dat, dey hold in their feelings. Dey don't talk bout the bothersome thangs, no sir," he shook his head. "dey put their family first and dats zactly what Mr. Benton did. His main priority was his ailing wife and getting her well…he suffered for her benefit and dats makes him a mighty fine man in my book."

"Mine, too," Miss Odessa agreed. "Dis town ought to be down on dey knees thanking him. The bank is gonna need a smart man to straighten thangs out when everythang blows over and it would serve everybody right ifing he jest threw up his hands and walked away."

"Benton would never do that, he has too much integrity." Kate smiled. "God has a way of working things out without our help. I pray for patience and strength and that He will take my worries away."

Standing at the door, shifting his hat from one hand to the other, Mr. Dodie pushed his thoughts of dread aside and nodded. "Dees last few months have brought bout pain and healing, dey have brought bout sorrow and hope for good thangs to come. We've seen the Lord's hand at every turn, but the funeral dis afternoon is gonna be a long, hard row to hoe. Folks don't seem to be willing to accept the facts. Dey are acting like a bunch of vipers ready to strike at anythang dat moves." He opened the back door. "My heart is heavy, Missus Kate, my heart is heavy."

"Mine too, Dodie," said Kate. "I hurt when my family hurts." She poured her untouched coffee down the sink. "Did I hear Little Missy slipping in early this morning, before daylight?"

"Yeah, she and Travis were out all night looking for James Everett," said Miss Odessa. "Poor thang, I reckon everybody's wailing and moaning over Hershel Tucker's corpse was more than the young boy could tolerate. No wonder he runned out of the funeral parlor faster than a streak of lightning. Problee seeking a hiding place for his soul, but I wish he'd come home."

Kate Carter bit her lip. "Mary Ruth must be beside herself. I understand why James Everett is so upset, but he needs to let his family and friends help him. It isn't good for him to suffer alone." She opened the cupboard door. "Odessa, do we need to…?"

"I know what you're gonna say and you don't need to worry. We gonna send food over, Miss Beff Anne baked a cake and Dodie is gonna deliver it."

"Yeah, I sho am, right after I finish with the chores. Little Missy has been out all night. She needs her rest, so I figure I'll do hers too."

"Thank you, Dodie. I can always count on you and Odessa. Y'all have been my backbone, holding me up, all these years. You've mourned with me and rejoiced with me, you've become a part of my life and I don't know what I'd do without you." Kate stood silent, searching for the right words. "I…"

"Dats enough," Dodie broke in. "You and yo family is all the family me and Odessa have." He shook his head. "We are family and family sticks together." He looked at his wife, waited for her to agree and then he was gone, out the door and down the back steps.

"Odessa," Kate's eyes brimmed with tears. "Dodie Frazier is a mighty fine man in my book."

"Yes, ma'am, in my book, too."

The early morning dimness didn't bother Miss Ella. She slowly made her way down the steps and followed the rope to the woodpile. She formed a pouch with her apron and piled it full with stove wood, but as she turned to leave she heard a slight shuffle. "Who's there?" she demanded. She cocked her head to the side and called out again, "Who's there? I feel your presence."

"It's me, Miss Ella," James Everett whispered.

"James Everett, is that you?"

"Yes, ma'am."

"Honey, what are you doing here? Don't you know your family is looking for you?"

"I figured they would be."

"Travis and Little Missy came here last night and they told me you were upset when you left the funeral home." Miss Ella gripped her apron with one hand and felt the air with the other. "Come, help me to the house. Are you all right?"

"Yes, ma'am, but I need to talk." He took her by the arm. "Do you have time?"

"Of course, you know I always have time for you." She smiled and allowed him to guide her to the porch and help her up the steps. "Travis said your mama is worried half to death about you? Where were you last night?"

"Under the trestle."

"You spent the night under the trestle?"

"Yes, ma'am."

"Why? You know that place is dangerous. Why are you hiding out? Why won't you go home?"

"Because I need to be alone. I need to sort things out."

"What kind of things?" Miss Ella waited until she heard the door open then she stepped inside and felt her way to the stove. She emptied her apron into the wood box and repeated, "What kind of things? I thought you would be relieved, now that we know the truth about your daddy but…but," she stuttered. "I hear a sadness in you voice. What is it? What's bothering you?" She counted the steps to the table and pulled out a chair then she sat down and ordered her guest to have a seat. "Tell me, James Everett, tell me."

The boy winched at her blind stare. He ducked his head, hiding his face, even though he knew she could not see his pain. Reluctantly, he slid into the chair across from her and peered up at her. "In my head, I keep hearing Mr. Tucker's voice calling Daddy a fool and a drunk and I hear Judge Wilkes and the mayor saying all those bad things about him." He tousled his hair. "They said he had no business snooping around Mr. Tucker's barn; he had no business hiding the books. They called him a sorry, lowdown drunk…and." He stopped, trying to decide if he should continue.

"Go on, get it all off your chest." Miss Ella encouraged. "I make no judgments. You and I are friends." Her voice softened.

"I can't understand why everybody is so willing to overlook a murderer and a thief." James Everett scooted to the edge of his chair. "People have looked down on Daddy for as long as I can remember, but he'd stopped his drinking and he died doing an admirable thing, but no one will give him credit for it. They just keep smearing his name. It ain't fair, Miss Ella, it ain't fair. Why can't they see that Daddy's life meant something? Why can't they see that his family loved him? I loved him." James Everett folded his arms defiantly "My daddy was guilty of a lot of things, but he was no murderer and he was no thief."

"I know, Honey, I know." Miss Ella reached out and rubbed the boy's arm. "It ain't fair that some folks are more blind than me. They see what they want to see and they cover up or deny the rest. It reminds me of the way Jesus was treated. But God knows the truth, we know the truth, and the Bible tells us that the truth will set us free. Stop worrying about what others think and concentrate on what you know to be the truth."

"But the truth is… my daddy was murdered and nobody is being held accountable for it." James Everett jumped up, almost knocking over his chair. "Mr. Tucker was such a coward, he should have been made to own up to his crime! He should be sitting in jail with Darby Brooks, he should be punished, but he took the easy way out." He slammed his fist down on the table. "It ain't fair, it ain't fair."

"No, it ain't fair, but you've got to listen to what I'm saying. Hershel Tucker ain't getting off easy, he ain't escaping justice. Don't you see?" She slowly rose from her chair. "He sealed his judgment day by committing suicide."

"Yes ma'am, I see that, but that don't take away the hurt he caused."

"That hurt can't be taken away. It never goes away completely, but you have to grieve before it will diminish."

"But, Miss Ella, I have been grieving…and it hurts…it hurts worse."

"That's because you're fueling the pain with anger." The old lady stepped away from the table. "I know what I'm talking about, James Everett. I was just a little older than you when my parents died and my aunt rejected me. I was angry for a long time and I nursed my resentment, I let it grow because being angry was easier than grieving. But I finally realized I was only putting off the hurt, I couldn't mend until I let go."

"But, how do I let go?"

"By opening your heart, not only to let the hurt out, but to let others in. I loved your daddy and so did your family. We're all hurting, we share your pain."

James Everett frowned thoughtfully. Miss Ella's statement made him realize his daddy's death was not his burden alone. Why hadn't he seen that before?

Chapter 20

Sheriff Connelly was convinced his prisoner would be safer if she were transported to the next county. He had ordered his deputy to rush the transfer paperwork over to the church, so he could sign them, but he had absolutely no intention of allowing Darby Brooks to attend the funeral services. This, in his opinion, would bring about the same result as an erupting volcano. He had spent the better part of the morning securing the church and gravesite and he did not intend to be swayed by Miss Brooks' pleading.

"But, Sheriff, please. I'm in shackles and handcuffs, what harm can I do?" Darby begged from the backseat of the deputy's car. "I just need to see Hershel one last time."

"You being here has already rubbed some folks the wrong way. Look at them staring at you." He motioned toward the crowd of gawkers standing on the walkway. "Ain't no way I'm going to let you walk into that church. And besides that, I don't see the logic in you wanting to say one last goodbye to someone you hate. All I've heard for the last few days is how he betrayed you and how much you despise him. Don't tell me, seeing his dead body is going to give you a change of heart."

"No, Sheriff, it isn't. I just need to see him, to try to wrap my head around why he wouldn't leave when I begged him to. I told him those kids would do us in, but he kept saying as long as the books were missing we had a chance."

"A chance to do what, Darby? Give the money back? To unkill Wiley Holloway?"

"No, I guess not. I'm not sure what he thought…he just seemed to give up. I don't think he cared anymore." Darby seemed genuinely sincere. "I think maybe he was sorry…I think he was having second thoughts."

"And what about you? Are you sorry?"

Darby's face grew sad; she spoke in a low, but distinct voice. "I'm sorry for a lot of things, but mostly, I'm sorry I ever came to this podunk little town." She looked at the sheriff with defiant eyes and stared in an unbroken silence until at last, he stepped back from the car and the deputy drove away.

"You were right in your decision to move her," Judge Wilkes called from the sidewalk. "We don't need to add to the fire, folks are already on edge."

"Yeah, we've got enough to worry about." Sheriff Connelly scanned the parking lot and shook his head. "Way too many people here already, it makes me uneasy."

"Me too, but what about the Holloway boy? Did you find him?"

"No, we searched during the night, but plan to look again after the funeral. I'm hoping he'll come home on his own."

The judge nodded. "He seems a little hotheaded, like his daddy."

"Oh, is that right?" The sheriff turned angrily. "I know James Everett and he's not hotheaded at all. He's just a young boy in a lot of pain. His daddy was murdered, Judge, have you forgotten that?"

Judge Wilkes lowered his head. He didn't answer because he thought maybe he had said enough already.

The two o'clock hour was fast approaching. The funeral director had the body in place and had arranged the flowers in double rows around the casket. The church was stuffed to full capacity; many people were leaning against the walls. Miss Ella, Travis and his family sat crowded together on the pew behind Kate Carter, her daughter and son-in-law. Little Missy chose to wait outside in hopes that James Everett would decide to attend. She wanted to talk to him, to make sure he was all right. Her thoughts of his suffering left her with an emptiness she could not measure.

"Are you waiting for James Everett?" Grady Dewberry asked as he sat down on the step next to her.

"Yes, sir. He didn't go home last night. Miss Ella said he was at her house this morning but he left and she doesn't know where he is."

"Do you think he'll come here?"

"I'm not sure. He's pretty upset." Little Missy twisted the hem of her dress. "He's ...he." She couldn't finish her sentence. She had no more words.

"I understand," Grady whispered softly. "Hurt and disappointment are hard emotions to overcome. I never knew my daddy, so I can only imagine how he must be feeling but I know disappointment and I know hurt."

"Are you talking about you and Mother? Grandmother told me you used to be in love with her."

"I was in love with Lizzy, I loved her very much and was deeply hurt when she rejected me. I acted a fool and said and did some mighty stupid things. I joined the army, met Tammy and asked her to marry me, but she turned me down. She said she was too young; she wasn't ready to be tied down." Grady hung his head. "Two rejections in less than two years really did a number on my self-confidence. I hurt so bad I didn't think I'd ever get over it, but I finally came to my senses."

"You don't love Mother anymore?" Little Missy asked.

"No, I still love her. I guess I always will, but I'm not in love with her anymore. I'm happy for Lizzy, I'm glad she married your father. He loves her...he's in love with her and she's in love with him." Grady whispered.

Little Missy looked up and smiled a weak smile.

"Love isn't always easy. Sometimes it hurts and disappoints, pretty much the way James Everett must be feeling."

"Yes, but I don't know how to help him. I don't know how to take away his hurt."

"Just be his friend, Katherine, that's all you can do." Grady stood up. "It's almost time, are you ready to go inside?"

"No, I think I'll wait here...just in case." Little Missy smoothed her dress as she watched him walk inside. Her thoughts were divided, at one time it would have made her mad to hear him admit to loving her mother, but now she wasn't offended by it. As a matter of fact, she found comfort in knowing he cared so deeply. True friendship is a combination of love and hurt. She understood that now, because James Everett was her friend, he was hurting and so was she.

The long-winded speeches given by Mayor Digby and Judge Wilkes, each trying to outdo the other, lengthened the service to almost two hours. Little Missy waited outside the whole time. She had no desire to sit and listen while Hershel Tucker was being glorified to the point of sainthood. Her stomach churned with an annoying wave of nausea each and every time Mr. Tucker's name was repeated. She thought she would surely keel over if she were forced to endure the mention of his name one more time. Her patience grew less and less as the service dragged on. It seemed an eternity but finally it came time for everyone to line up behind the hearse and solemnly make the long walk to the gravesite. Little Missy joined her family and watched the pallbearers slide the coffin from the back of the long, black limousine and carry the body the short distance between the graves. Pastor Shaddix encouraged the widely spaced crowd to step closer and then he read the scripture, "For all that is in the world, the lust of the flesh, the lust of the eyes, and the pride of life, is not from the Father, but is from the world." He closed his Bible and looked at the crowd. There were so many people he did not recognize. So many unfamiliar faces, he wondered who they were and why they were there. He hesitated with great conviction, pondering if he should request that only close friends remain for the final interment. The tension in the atmosphere, similar to that of someone blindfolded and standing in front of a firing squad, had derailed the solemn occasion and made the pastor reluctant to continue but after a quick assessment of the time already invested he decided it would be best to finish as quickly as possible.

"From dust man was created and to dust he will return." He raised his eyes toward heaven and started to pray but he stopped when, from the corner of his eye, he caught a glimpse of James Everett walking from the edge of the cemetery with a shotgun over his shoulder. His sudden unanticipated reaction caused everyone to turn around.

The people were astonished. They stood in breathless silence, watching him come closer and closer. No one made any attempt to stop him or to investigate his motives; they just simply watched until he reached the outer circle, then they stepped aside and allowed him to approach the open grave.

The judge glanced at the mayor. "Isn't that the Holloway kid?" he whispered.

"Yes." The mayor nodded. "What's he going to do with that gun?"

Both men turned their attention to the sheriff, waiting for him to do something.

Sheriff Connelly stepped forward. "Son, what are you doing here?"

"Miss Ella said I should share my hurt." James Everett breathed heavily and searched the crowd for his family. He found his mother and nodded. She moved toward him, but Travis stopped her. "Let him speak, Mama," he whispered and then he gave his little brother an endearing look.

Encouraged by this, James Everett raised his voice. "I've come here to have my say."

"Okay." The sheriff steadied his voice. "But give me the gun before somebody gets hurt."

"Ain't nobody gonna get hurt, Sheriff. It ain't loaded. I only brung it here cause I wanted everybody to see it." James Everett held it up high so the people in the back could see and then he unbreeched it and carefully handed it to the sheriff. The sheriff examined it and then passed it on to Travis.

"That's a .410 single shot shotgun and it belonged to my daddy," James Everett continued, his voice trembling with a mixture of anger and resentment. "He handed it down to me on my last birthday cause he said all boys need a good squirrel gun. He showed me how to shoot it and he taught me how to be safe. And this here…" His hands shook as he pulled a chain out from around his neck. "This is my daddy's military dog tag. It says, Private Wiley Eugene Holloway, US Army." He smiled proudly and wiped his nose with the back of his hand. "Daddy said he was a young man when he went to war, but he come out old beyond his years. He said the killing and suffering he witnessed hardened him, but in spite of all that, he said he was proud of his service to our country." James Everett met his mother's gaze. "I was proud of him, too, and so was Mama. She gave me Daddy's dog tag on the day we buried him because she said she knew he would want me to have it." The young boy sniffed and angrily wiped his nose again. He was determined to finish his speech, so he suppressed his anguish, stood on his tiptoes and pointed up the hill. "Daddy's grave is over yonder, the one with the homemade marker. We don't have a headstone yet, but me and Travis and Jo Nell have started a fund so we can buy him a real nice marble one."

Mary Ruth Holloway blinked back the tears and smiled. Travis put his arm around her and nodded toward his brother, coaxing him on.

"And one last thing." James Everett shoved his hand deep into his pocket. "This is Daddy's ten dollar gold piece." He rubbed the coin down the front of his shirt and then spread his palms wide. "It ain't real," he said, flipping it over to show the inscription. "It says, A man's soul is worth more than gold." James Everett swallowed hard and took several deep breaths. "Daddy showed this to me one time when he was coming off of a drunk. He was sitting on the back porch with his head bent, silently staring at it as if it was of great value. I asked him what he was doing and he told me he was taking stock of his life. He said he knew he was a big disappointment and that he hadn't made much of himself but the coin brought him comfort." James Everett closed his hand and put the coin back into his pocket. "Daddy explained that the words written on the back reminded him that God loved him even when he didn't feel loveable." The boy turned full circle, staring into the faces of the people standing around him. "Daddy admitted he had a weakness for liquor and he said he wished he could go back to before he ever took his first drink. He said things would be different." James Everett's voice faltered and the tears came. He could hold them back no longer. They streamed down his face. "My daddy was not perfect, but I loved him and that's why I'm here today. I want y'all to see him, the way he really was. He had his faults, but he wasn't a bad person." James Everett sucked in a deep breath and blew it out slowly. He wiped his eyes and then looked directly at the mayor and Judge Wilkes. "Daddy had changed, he'd quit his drinking and he was trying real hard. Why can't y'all see his life was worth something? He died trying to do the right thing. Why do y'all make excuses for Hershel Tucker and vilify Wiley Holloway?" He shook his head. "My daddy might have been a drunk, but he wasn't a murderer and he wasn't a thief." James Everett hung his head and cried aloud. His tears dropped to the ground.

The crowd stood still and quiet. Nobody moved except to exchange uncomfortable glances with the person standing next to them. The depth of James Everett's feelings spilled out and caused a sense of conviction, leaving everyone speechless, even the pastor. He offered no words of comfort, just a sympathetic stare.

Finally, Little Missy slipped from beside her grandmother and stood next to her friend. "Your daddy sounds like a very nice man, James Everett, I wish I had met him." She locked her arm in his and stood tall and defiant.

James Everett squeezed her hand and slowly raised his head. He looked at all the staring eyes, the blank faces of the people familiar and unfamiliar to him and then he summoned his last ounce of pride. "I've had my say now, do with it what you will." He then stepped forward. Little Missy fell in behind him and led the way for Travis, Miss Ella, the Holloway and the Carter family. One by one the rest of the crowd dispersed until only the pastor and the undertaker remained.

Chapter 21

The days that followed were like a vapor, blending together and then vanishing away. It would have been hard for Little Missy to distinguish one day from another had it not been for her precious cat calendar. The turning of the page brought the excitement of Labor Day and a picture of the yellow cat lying lazily next to a picnic table draped with the American flag. The annual celebration was an event talked about and looked forward to by the entire community. The creek area underneath the trestle had been transformed from the local swimming hole to an extravagant array of picnic tables, large umbrellas and volleyball nets. Several tents, hosting the judges' tables for the horseshoe tournament, the best pie contest and the pickle and spice display, had been erected along the path leading to the big rock. The creek bank was dotted with beach towels and quilts and dozens of eager swimmers.

Little Missy was excited about the celebration. The tide had finally turned and her life was becoming calm and stable. She felt close to God again. She realized He had been listening to her prayers all along and He had answered them. Her mother was healing, becoming more and more like her old self. She seemed happy again, in spite of all the things that had happened. Her father and Mr. Boggs had been able to straighten out the accounting discrepancies and he had settled into the big office at the bank. Ivy Holcomb was complimentary of his professionalism and banking skills and the employees were respectful. Although, many of the customers still viewed him as uppity, he was hopeful that in time, even if they didn't change their opinion they would at least, warm up to him.

The biggest change was with James Everett. He was more free-spirited, less burdened by resentment and ready to let go of the old and concentrate on the new. He had confided to Little Missy that his soul was at peace now, and he and his family intended to honor his daddy's memory no matter what others thought. They were thankful that foreclosure was no longer a threat and they were praying that Travis would be able to attend Bible college next spring.

Little Missy stood on the hill and contemplated the fact that summer was about to come to an end. It seemed bittersweet that today would mark the beginning and the end of a time of revelation and recovery. The last few months had been eventful. It was only fitting that she took a few moments to reflect before joining her family.

Mr. Dodie and Miss Odessa were attending to their famous mouthwatering barbeque ribs. Grandmother Kate and Elizabeth Anne were busy at the contest signup table and Benton was watching the crew attach the final addition to the fireworks display. Little Missy found it difficult to recognize her father at first because her mother had insisted he wear a casual pullover instead of his usual dress shirt and tie. She felt it was more appropriate for a barbeque and that it would indeed, make him seem less uppity and more identifiable with the common man.

Little Missy mused at the beehive-like activity. People were scurrying about, seemingly enjoying the festivities, but oblivious to what was going on around them.

Travis and Peggy were standing near the sandbar watching the younger children play. Grady Dewberry was helping Miss Ella out of his truck and James Everett and his friends were swimming in the middle of the creek. The water looked cool and inviting but Little Missy wasn't interested in swimming, she wanted to join Sadie and the other girls on the big rock.

Mayor Digby was at the podium, trying to make announcements but his voice was muffled by the thunderous sound of the speeding freight train fast approaching the trestle. Little Missy felt the rumble of the train as she made her way toward the rock. She remembered the time when the cloud of dust showered down on Sadie and her friends so she hesitated and took cover under the large shade tree at the edge of the trail. The minute the engine got to the trestle the sound grew louder…louder than she remembered. The creaking and popping of the wooden beams and the sound of squealing rails sent a chill up her back, so she covered her ears and looked at the crowd.

At first, no one paid attention but soon the noise was too loud to ignore. They all gazed up and watched a plume of dust fill the air. Sadie and Donna Jo grabbed their blankets and darted toward the shade tree, but Carrie searched for her shoes. An updraft of wind scattered the dust cloud and exposed the horrifying view of the weak support beams being bent and bowed to the point of break. The weight and movement of the boxcars shook the rails violently until suddenly one of the support beams snapped in two and splashed into the water. Then, like a row of dominoes, another beam snapped and then another, causing the iron trestle to sway. It teetered to the left and then to the right, tilting until several of the boxcars slid off the track and slipped between the iron girders. The engine screeched its breaks and jerked to a halt.

"Get out of the water!" someone yelled. "Move, move, get out now!"

The warning sent everyone into a panic, but it came too late. The weight of the suspended train cars pulled the engine backward, unhooked several boxcars and catapulted them straight down into the water. A tidal wave rose up and slammed down hard, sweeping the swimmers and everybody in the water downstream in a violent rush. James Everett and his friends fought to keep their heads above the waves. The swift current knocked Travis, Peggy and the children off their feet and sent them helplessly into the menacing flood. Screams and cries for help filled the air.

Every able-bodied person rushed to the water's edge. Benton and Grady dove in and started pulling people out. Travis and Peggy franticly swam toward each child, grabbed them one by one and then rushed them to the safety of their parents' arms. But Mrs. Hudson's arms were empty. Her child was still in the creek.

"There's Tess," she screamed, pointing to her three-year-old. The raging current was pushing her further and further away, carrying her terrified cries with her. "Please, save my baby!"

Travis quickly dove back into the water and swam toward the little girl.

James Everett and the other boys crawled out of the creek, exhausted and gasping for breath.

"Are you all right?" Mr. Langford sat down beside him. He, too, was exhausted from the many trips in and out of the water.

"Yes sir, I think so." James Everett breathed deeply.

"Good," Benton answered. "Do you know where Katherine is?"

"Little Missy, uh…no sir. Do you want me to look for her?"

"No, I'll go, but you and your friends need to move to higher ground." He pointed. "It's too dangerous here."

One side of the trestle had dropped down several feet and was hanging in the air.

Benton scrambled up the bank and franticly called for his daughter. He was relieved when he saw her and her friends rushing toward him.

"Father, Father," she called.

"Are you okay?" he asked.

"Yes, but Carrie is hurt. She's unconscious. She got caught on the rock and was knocked down by the huge wave. I think she hit her head. She's bleeding."

"Go find Dr. Whatley," Benton ordered. "I'll check on her."

"Yes sir," she answered, turning immediately to obey.

"And you girls," he pointed to Donna Jo and Sadie, "go find her parents and bring them too."

"Yes sir," they answered in unison.

As Benton rushed up the path he could see that several more beams had collapsed and were being slapped against the concrete pylons. Each shockwave threaten to topple the weakened structure. The slightest movement could bring it straight down, crashing across the rock.

Dr. Whatley and Carrie's parents followed the girls to the shade tree. Grandmother Kate rushed to Little Missy's side. Elizabeth Anne joined them. She buried her face into her hands and prayed silently. She was consumed with nervous tension, afraid to move, afraid to speak, afraid the next cracking sound would bring disaster.

Slowly Benton inched his way across the narrow earthen bridge, creeping closer and closer toward the rock, but suddenly he heard a long, low, collapsing sound. He looked up. The iron trestle tilted to the side and started to roll over. Crossties broke loose and splashed loudly into the water. Gravel and another thick cloud of dust filled the air.

Benton knew his life was at risk, but he could not leave Carrie. A twinge of panic sent him rushing forward, covering his head to protect against the falling gravel. Shouts of warning came from below.

With one last groan, the structure turned upside down and fell with tremendous speed, dragging the rest of the train with it. Debris and dirt mixed with the large splash of water and formed a blindfold, blocking the view, hiding the twisted, tangled metal and shards of rock as they crashed to the bottom of the creek.

Screams of terror and horrified cries intensified until there was nothing but silence. Stunned and uncertain of what to do, the crowd stood statue-like. With bated breath, they waited and waited, hoping to see movement when the cloud finally dissipated, but there was no hope. The rock was gone, submerged under the water with the rest of the wreckage. There was no possibility of survival.

Carrie's mother threw herself into the arms of her husband. She was inconsolable. Her only child was gone. She raised her tear-filled eyes toward Elizabeth Anne and tried to speak, tried to convey her sorrow. She wanted to pledge her undying gratitude, but from far away she heard a shout, a man's voice calling…"Here, we're here," he shouted. "We're all here."

Everybody turned. Benton Langford was walking out of the water and he was carrying Carrie. She was conscious and waving. And a few yards down stream from them was Travis. He was holding baby Tess. They were all alive and well.

Chapter 22

Little Missy looked out the window of the upstairs bedroom in the Richardson Estate and pondered what living in this winding staircase, parlor-less, grand mansion was going to be like. This would become her room when the renovations were completed. Her mother and father were downstairs going over the plans with Mr. Mizzell, the contractor. Her reluctance to move from her grandmother's house still loomed in the back of her mind, but her mother's laughter and excited chatter brought a sense of well being, as if it was meant to be. It seemed as if God was personally watching over her, blessing her in so many ways she couldn't even count. Not only had her father become her hero on Labor Day but he had also become a welcomed member of the community. Carrie's father, a man who had never had anything to do with banks before, had marched into the First State Bank the next day and had opened his first bank account. He had proclaimed that Benton Langford's actions had proved him to be a man of character, one deserving respect and honor. He publicly apologized and that, in turn, had opened the door for many others, some of which included the members of the Board of Directors, the judge and the mayor. Folks no longer turned the other way when they met him on the street; instead they addressed him as Ben and stopped to make polite conversation.

Mrs. Hudson had shown her appreciation toward Travis by forcing him to accept a donation of one hundred dollars toward his college fund. She said her daughter's life was worth so much more than that and the least she could do was to make a monetary donation toward a worthy cause.

The Central Freight Company had sent a multitude of their top executives to investigate the tragedy. They had mourned the death of their employees and had pledged to make sure nothing like that would ever happen again. Their recovery crews and divers were disassembling the trestle and making preparations to lift the train out of the water. Several groups of engineers, welders and construction people had taken up residence in the company's hastily constructed city of tents near the creek bank. They would live there for as long as it took to rebuild a safe and sturdy trestle.

"So, what do you think?" Benton stuck his head inside the doorway. "Can you be happy here?"

Little Missy turned around and nodded.

"Are you sure?"

"Yes, sir. Mother seems to be happy and you can see the bank from here. You can walk to work."

Benton walked to the window and looked out. "Yes, indeed, I can walk to work but..." He frowned. "The sheriff is driving up the driveway...you haven't been trespassing again, have you?"

"The sheriff?" Little Missy was surprised. "No sir, I haven't been trespassing."

"Good." Her father's mouth curved into a smile. "Let's go find out what he wants."

Little Missy ran ahead of her father and opened the door. They watched Sheriff Connelly retrieve a bundle from the trunk of his police car and swiftly make his way up the porch steps.

"What brings you here this morning, Sheriff? I hope it isn't official business." Benton stepped outside.

"No, not official...but." The sheriff shrugged his shoulders. "I thought you might be interested in seeing this." He laid the bundle down and carefully unwrapped it. "The divers brought this up from the bottom of the creek."

"What is it?" Little Missy's curiosity sparked.

"It's a golden candlestick." Sheriff Connelly held it up.

"Is it Yolanda Richardson's golden candlestick? Is it the one she used to kill her husband?"

"Could be," the sheriff answered. "There was never enough evidence against her, just a lot of speculations and wild stories, but even after twenty years, I suspect the stories are true."

Little Missy's mind started to spin. "It's a mystery...a mystery that needs to be solved." She rubbed her hands together.

"Now, little lady, don't you go getting any ideas." The sheriff gave her a warning stare. "I don't want you snooping around, getting into trouble again."

"Oh, no sir," Little Missy answered, her eyes shiny with excitement. "I don't intend on getting into trouble." She adjusted her facial expression, trying to look innocent. "I've learned my lesson." She said the words aloud but in the back of her mind she silently whispered, "I can't wait to tell James Everett."

www.ingramcontent.com/pod-product-compliance
Lightning Source LLC
Chambersburg PA
CBHW071734080526
44588CB00013B/2024